W9-BGZ-180

W9-BGZ-180

letterhead & logo
DESIGN **6**

ROCKPORT

Consent of the artists concerned and no responsibility are accepted by producer,
publisher, or printer for any infringement of copyright or otherwise, arising
from the contents of this publication. Every effort has been made to ensure
that credits accurately comply with information supplied.

First published in the United States of America by
Rockport Publishers, Inc.
33 Commercial Street
Gloucester, Massachusetts 01930-5089
Telephone: (978) 282-9590
Facsimile: (978) 283-2742

Distributed to the book trade and
art trade in the United States by
North Light Books, an imprint of
F & W Publications
1507 Dana Avenue
Cincinnati, Ohio 45207
Telephone: (800) 289-0963

Other distribution by
Rockport Publishers, Inc.
Gloucester, Massachusetts 01930-5089

ISBN 1-56496-618-6

10 9 8 7 6 5 4 3

Design: Stoltze Design
Front cover images:
(top left) Designer: That's Cadiz! Orignials, client: Bicycle Club of Seattle
(bottom left) Designer: Acro Media, Inc., client: Acro Media, Inc.
(right) Designer: Synergy Design, client: Mirador Pictures
Back cover images:
(top left) Designer: Henderson Tyner Art Co., client: Pam Fish
(top right) Designer: Korn Design, client: Hooch & Holly's Restaurant
(bottom) Designer: Kirimia Design, client: Kirimia Design Office

Printed in China.

letterhead &
logo
DESIGN 6

GLOUCESTER MASSACHUSETTS

ROCKPORT PUBLISHERS

6

DESIGN

intro
duction

An effective logo speaks directly and instantly. A logo, unlike a multi-page
brochure or even a poster, must deliver the goods with minimal means.
Well designed logos deliver the message and the essence of the business
they represent. A letterhead system allows the designer a wider breadth of
possibilities: clever printing techniques and the use of paper distinguish
the most unique and dynamic systems.

In making this book, we opened hundreds of envelopes and sifted through
countless submissions: in them we discovered the diverse range of logos,
letterheads, envelopes, business cards, disk stickers, and packaging labels
that fill this book with thoughtful and sophisticated work.

We probably could have filled the whole book with Art Chantry's handcrafted
and streetwise logos. Avoiding digital means entirely, Chantry proves once
again that good design is about good ideas, not the latest computer program.

Carlos Segura integrates [T-26]'s artistic and contemporary typefaces
with traditional letterpress techniques to create well-crafted and dynamic
letterhead pieces.

Hornall Anderson Design Works delivered an array of work for creative and professional services that incorporated a classic and refined use of typography and imagery.

We received submissions from all over the world—and found that sensitive typography, more than anything else, distinguishes a good logo or letterhead from a bad one. In the original printed material, the various weights and rich textures of the papers satisfied the sense of touch, as well as design challenges. Through embossing, die cutting, and letterpressing, the featured designers celebrated the letterhead as an object passed from one person to another.

We hope you find inspiration in this collection of fresh new work from many of today's best creatives.

– Chris Reese & Clifford Stoltze
Stoltze Design

STOLTZE
D E S I G N ,   I N C .

Stoltze Design was established in Boston in 1984 by Clifford Stoltze. Over the past fifteen years, the multi-dimensional studio has evolved into a ten-person team of creative and business personnel. Preferring not to specialize, the studio has worked with a diverse group of clients, ranging from the software to the entertainment industry, including Fidelity Investments, Lotus, Nokia, Houghton Mifflin, Capitol Records, and Lego toys. An avid music enthusiast, Clif Stoltze is also a partner in the Boston-based independent record label, Castle von Buhler, designing all of the packaging as well as co-producing some of the projects. This has led to assignments for record labels as diverse as Matador and Windham Hill. Stoltze Design's work includes identities, collateral, publications, packaging, and website design.

Recognized for their innovative design solutions and expressive typography, Stoltze has received numerous awards from national design organizations some of which include the American Institute of Graphic Arts (AIGA), the American Center for Design, the Society of Publication Designers (SPD), and the Type Directors Club.

Published work appears in **Graphic Design America, Graphis Annual Reports, Typograhics 2 Cybertype** and most recently in **Communication Arts, Print** magazine, and in a June 1998 **How** magazine article, and **CD Design: Breaking the Sound Barrier.** Exhibited internationally in shows, Stoltze's work is also in the permanent collection of the Cooper Hewitt, National Design Museum.

logo and promotional folder
REYNOLDS DEWALT
printer

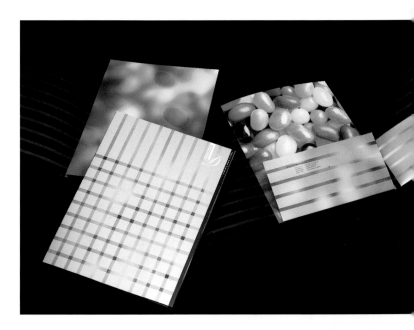

PLANETINTERACTIVE

identity system
PLANET INTERACTIVE
new media design group

identity system
OFFICE ENVIRONMENTS
office furniture dealer

logo
CASTLE VON BUHLER RECORDS
Splashdown (electro pop band)

identity system
FIRST SENSE
computer software company

wpa
LONDON

Walker Thomas Associates

Catherine Thomas
Design Director

Walker Thomas Associates
Melbourne Pty Ltd
Design Consultants

Top Floor, Osment Building
Maples Lane, Prahran
Victoria 3181 Australia

Walker Pinfold

with compliments

KENNEDY

fax (515) 243

professional
services

SERVICE
800.659.0898

EMAIL
steepco@aol.com
steepco@juno.com

WWW
www.steep.com

ONE AND ONLY TEA MATCHBOX

PO BOX 89 SOUTH GLASTONBURY, CT 06073 USA

800 STEEPCO

steep

PREMIUM LEAF TEAS & HIGH-IMPACT COCOAS™

design firm | Plum Notion Design Laboratory
designers | Damion Silver, Jeff Piazza
client | Steep Tea

design firm	Studio Hill
art director	Sandy Hill
designers	Sandy Hill, Emma Roberts-Wilson
client	Meyners + Co.
tools	Quark XPress, Macintosh
paper/printing	Strathmore Elements/ Black + Zhits Opaque White and Metallic Ink Temboss and Round Cornering

design firm	Hornall Anderson Design Works, Inc.
art director	Jack Anderson
designers	Jack Anderson, Debra McCloskey,
	Holly Finlayson
client	Personify
tool	Macromedia FreeHand

design firm	Studio Hill
art director	Sandy Hill
designer	Emma Roberts-Wilson
client	Tech 2 Me
tools	Adobe Illustrator, Macintosh

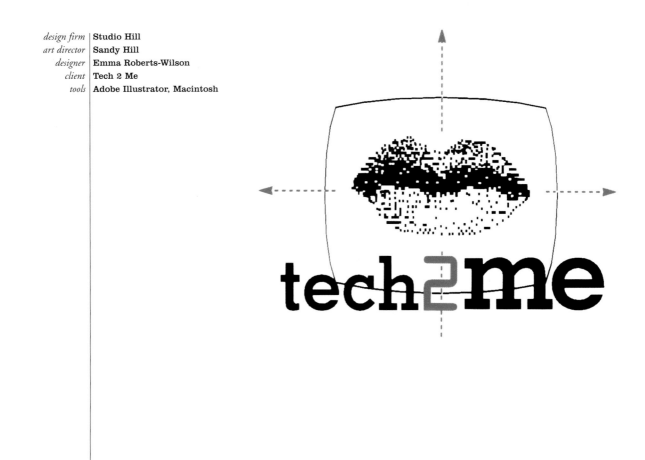

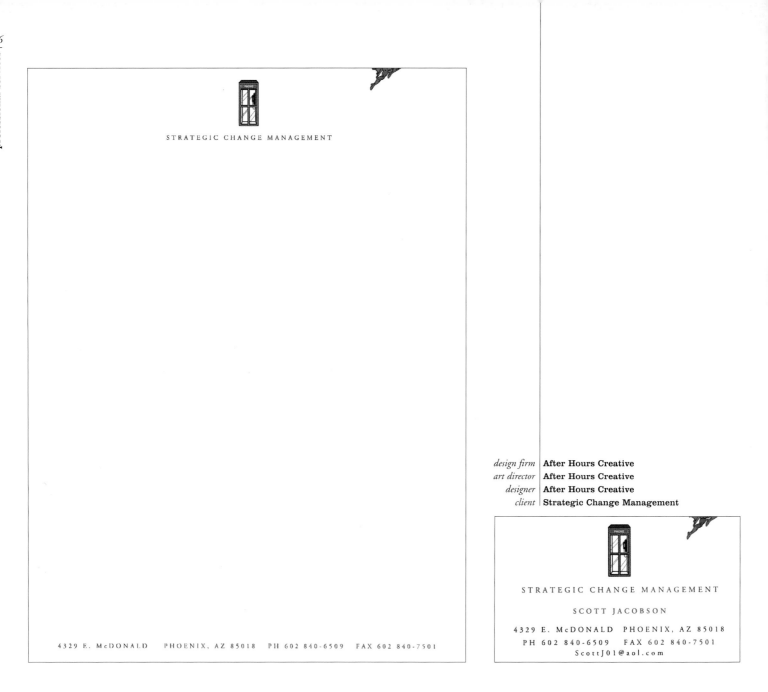

STRATEGIC CHANGE MANAGEMENT

4329 E. McDONALD   PHOENIX, AZ 85018   PH 602 840-6509   FAX 602 840-7501

design firm | **After Hours Creative**
art director | **After Hours Creative**
designer | **After Hours Creative**
client | **Strategic Change Management**

STRATEGIC CHANGE MANAGEMENT

SCOTT JACOBSON

4329 E. McDONALD   PHOENIX, AZ 85018
PH 602 840-6509   FAX 602 840-7501
ScottJ01@aol.com

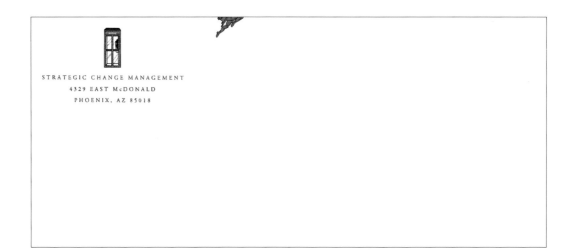

STRATEGIC CHANGE MANAGEMENT
4329 EAST McDONALD
PHOENIX, AZ 85018

design firm	Bob's Haus
designer	Bob Dahlquist
client	Bruce Whitelam, Whitelam + Whitelam
tools	Macromedia FreeHand 5.5, Macintosh Quadra 800
paper/printing	Classic Crest/Lithography

design firm	Bob's Haus
designer	Bob Dahlquist
client	Bruce Benning
tools	Macromedia FreeHand 5.5, Adobe Photoshop 4, Macintosh G3
paper/printing	Classic Crest/Lithography

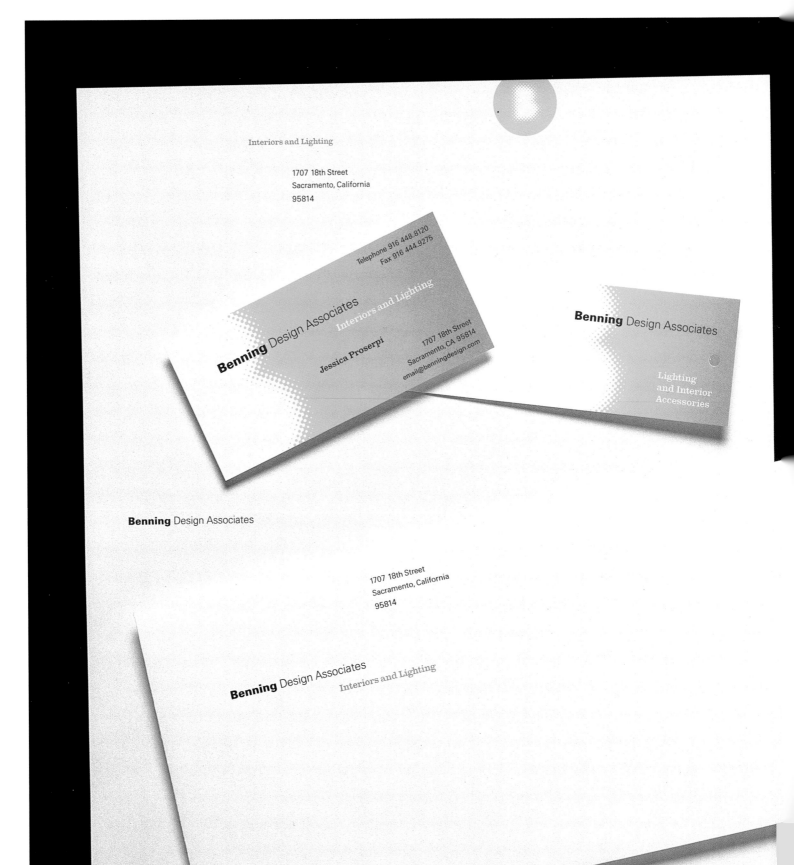

innoVisions™

design firm | Hornall Anderson Design Works, Inc.
art director | Jack Anderson
designers | Jack Anderson, Kathy Saito, Alan Copeland
client | Wells Fargo
tool | Macromedia FreeHand

design firm | Hornall Anderson Design Works, Inc.
art director | Jack Anderson
designers | Jack Anderson, Kathy Saito, Alan Copeland
client | Wells Fargo
tool | Macromedia FreeHand
paper/printing | 70 lb. Mohawk Superfine, Bright White Text

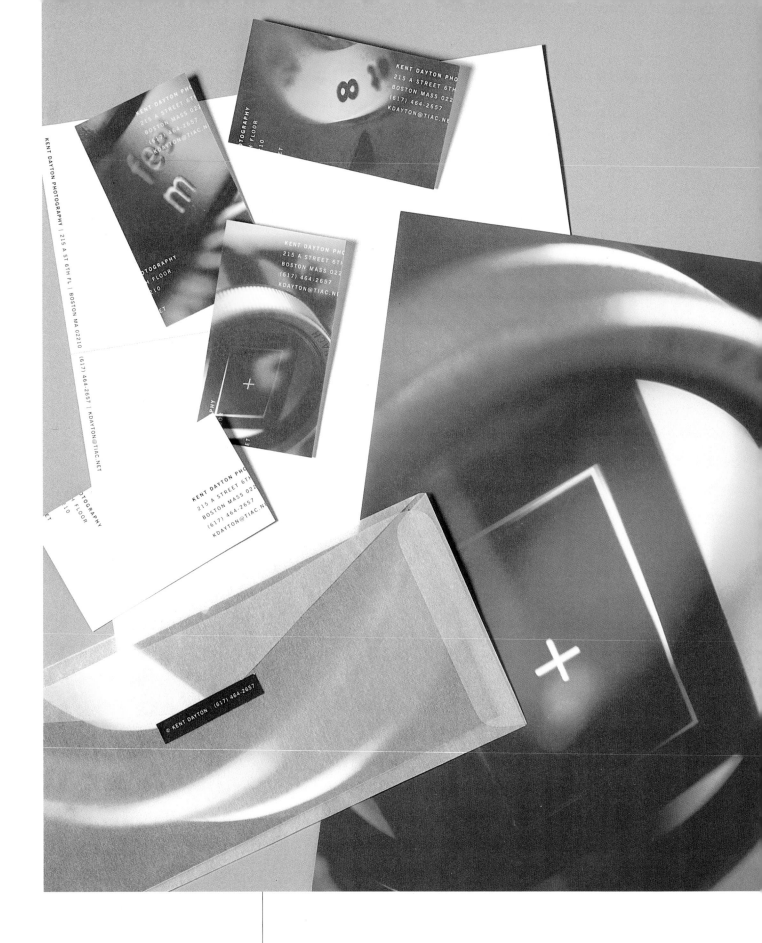

design firm | **Visual Dialogue**
art director | **Fritz Klaetke**
designer | **Fritz Klaetke**
client | **Kent Dayton**
tools | **Quark XPress, Adobe Photoshop, Macintosh Power PC**
paper/printing | **Mohawk/Shear Color Printing**

design firm	Vrontikis Design Office
art director	Petrula Vrontikis
designer	Logo and Stationary: Susan Carter
client	Levene, Neale, Bender and Rankin, L.L.P.
tools	Adobe Illustrator, Quark XPress
paper/printing	Neenah Classic Crest/Coast Lithographics

design firm	Studio Bubblan
art director	Kari Palmquist
designers	Jeanette Palmquist, Kari Palmquist
client	MA Arkitekter
tools	Macromedia FreeHand, Quark XPress
paper/printing	Storafine/Etcetera Offset

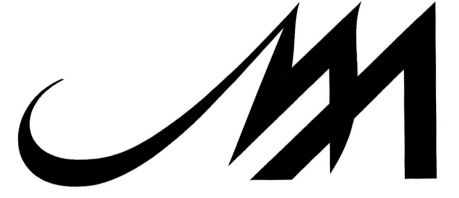

JASNA

JANE AUSTEN SOCIETY
OF NORTH AMERICA

ELSA A. SOLENDER
President

BARBARA HELLERING
Vice President

GISELE RANKIN
Secretary

GEORGE BRANTZ
Treasurer

NILI OLAV
Assitant Treasurer

BARBARA LARKIN
*Membership Secretary-
United States*

NANCY THURSTON
*Membership Secretary-
Canada*

RENEE CHARRON
Treasurer-Canada

LEE RIDGEWAY
Publications Secretary

design firm | **Grafik Communications, Ltd.**
designers | **Kristin Moore, Richard Hamilton,**
Judy Kirpich
client | **Jasna**
tool | **Quark XPress 3.3**

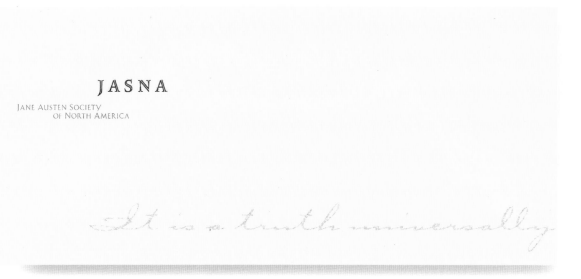

JASNA

JANE AUSTEN SOCIETY
OF NORTH AMERICA

design firm	Nielinger Kommunikations design
art director	Nielinger Kommunikations design
designer	Christian Nielinger
paper/printing	Gohrsurühle, Zanders/Two color

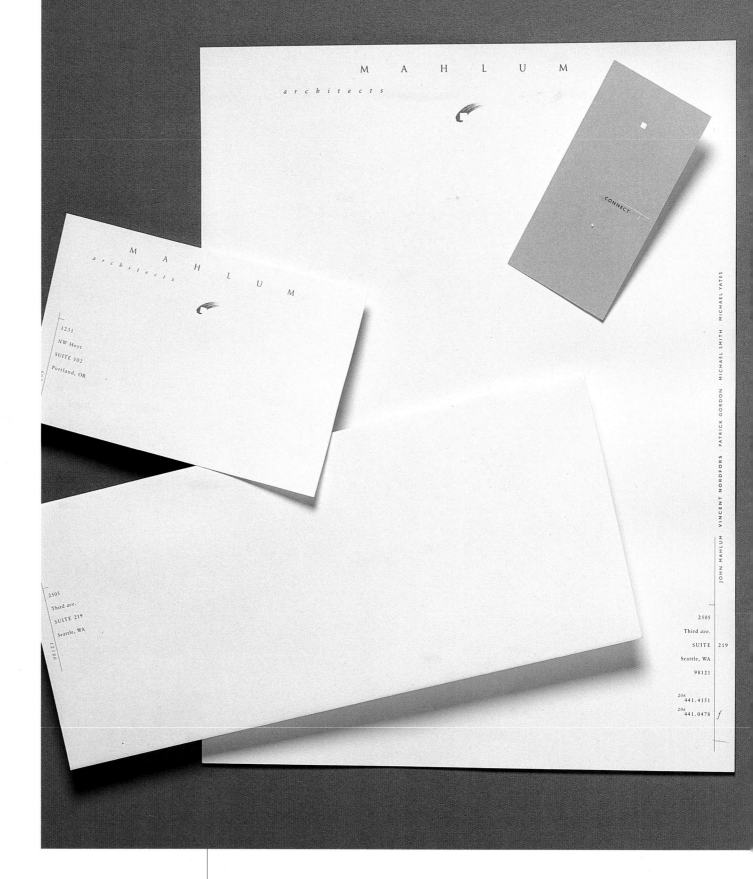

design firm	Hornall Anderson Design Works, Inc.
art director	Jack Anderson
designers	Jack Anderson, Heidi Favour, Margaret Long
client	Mahlum
tool	Macromedia FreeHand
paper/printing	Mohawk Superfine Recycled White

design firm	Vanderbyl Design
art director	Michael Vanderbyl
designers	Michael Vanderbyl, Amanda Fisher
client	Rocket Science
tool	Adobe Illustrator 7
paper/printing	Starwhite Vicksburg/Expressions litho

design firm Sayles Graphic Design
art director John Sayles
designer John Sayles
client Big Daddy Photography
tool Macintosh
paper/printing Classic Crest Natural White/Offset

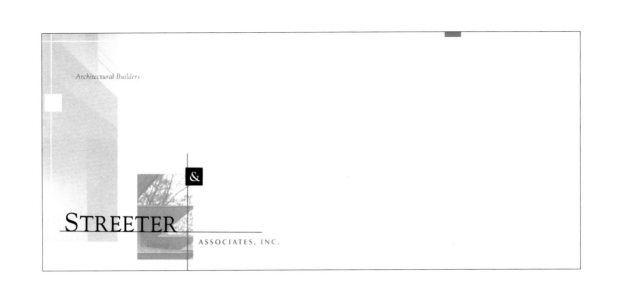

design firm | Design Center
art director | John Reger
designer | Sherwin Schwartzrock
client | Streeter & Associates, Inc.
tools | Macromedia FreeHand, Macintosh
paper/printing | Classic Crest/Pro Craft

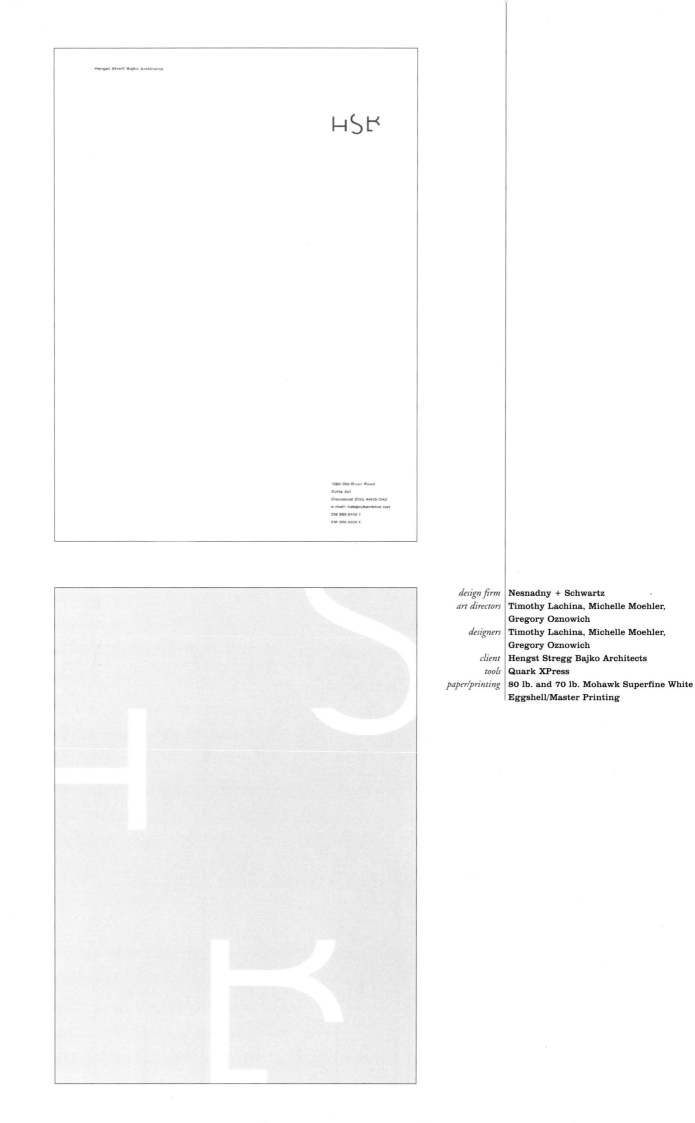

Hengst Streff Bajko Architects

HSB

1280 Old River Road
Suite 201
Cleveland Ohio 44113-1243
e-mail: hsb@cyberdrive.net
216 566 0440 l
216 566 0229 t

design firm	Nesnadny + Schwartz
art directors	Timothy Lachina, Michelle Moehler, Gregory Oznowich
designers	Timothy Lachina, Michelle Moehler, Gregory Oznowich
client	Hengst Stregg Bajko Architects
tools	Quark XPress
paper/printing	80 lb. and 70 lb. Mohawk Superfine White Eggshell/Master Printing

design firm	Vanderbyl Design
art director	Michael Vanderbyl
designer	Michael Vanderbyl
client	Archetype
tool	Quark XPress
paper/printing	Starwhite Vicksburg/Archetype

MARK CAMPBELL
president

ARCHETYPE | A PRINTING COLLABORATIVE
75 SHIELDS COURT · UNIT 7
MARKHAM, ONTARIO · L3R 9T4
TEL:905·479·2009 | FAX:905·479·7669

arche_type

profe

Walker Pinfold Associates

wpa
LONDON

Walker Thomas Associates

Catherine Thomas
Design Director

Walker Thomas Associates
Melbourne Pty Ltd
Design Consultants

Top Floor, Osment Building
Maples Lane, Prahran
Victoria 3181 Australia
T 03 9521 4433
F 03 9521 4466
E wta@creativeaccess.com.au

Walker Pinfold Associates

with compliments

Associated Office

Walker Pinfold Associates
London Limited
Design Consultants

Walker Thomas Associates
Melbourne Pty Ltd
Design Consultants

17 The Ivories
6 Northampton Street
London N1 2HY

Top Floor, Osment Building
Maples Lane, Prahran
Victoria 3181

T 0171 354 5887
F 0171 354 0319
E wpalondon@aapi.co.uk

T 03 9521 4433
F 03 9521 4466
E wta@creativeaccess.com.au

Walker Pinfold Associates
London Limited
Design Consultants

17 The Ivories
6 Northampton Street
London N1 2HY

T 0171 354 5887
F 0171 354 0319
E wpalondon@aapi.co.uk

Reg. in England No. 238 4906

Associated Office

Walker Thomas Associates
Melbourne Pty Ltd
Design Consultants

Top Floor, Osment Building
Maples Lane, Prahran
Victoria 3181

T 03 9521 4433
F 03 9521 4466
E wta@creativeaccess.com.au

A.C.N. 066 086 888

design firm	**After Hours Creative**
art director	**After Hours Creative**
designer	**After Hours Creative**
client	**enx**

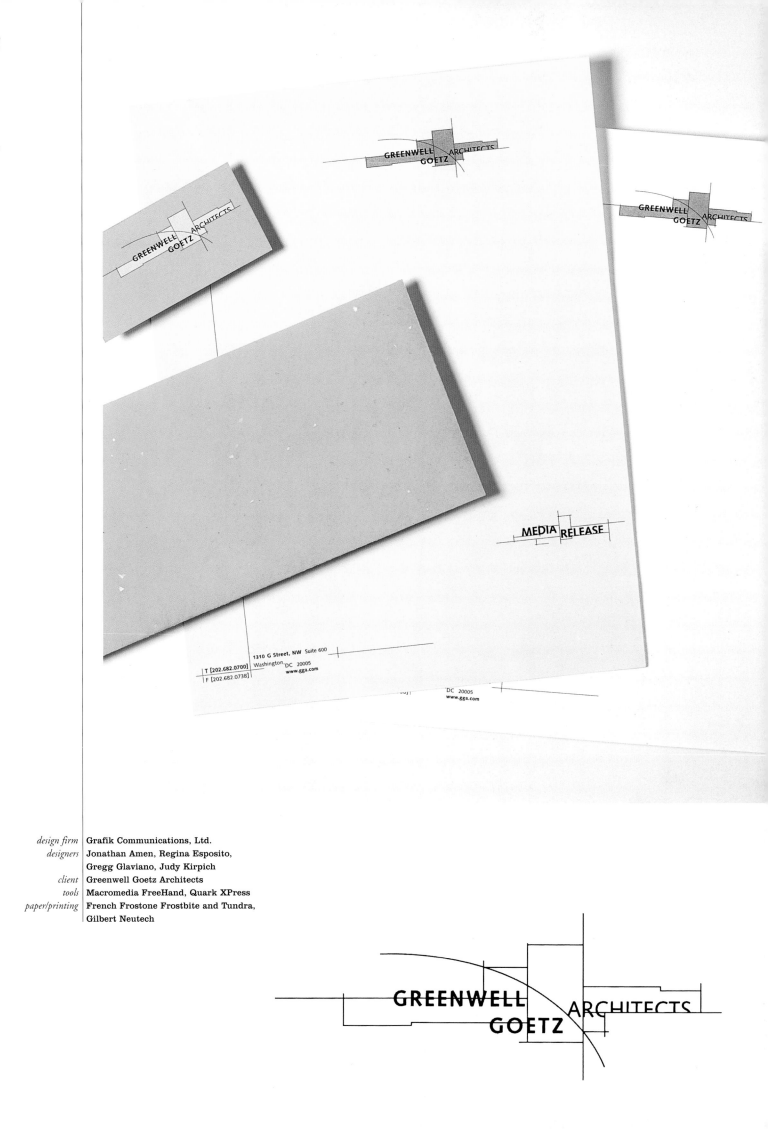

design firm	Grafik Communications, Ltd.
designers	Jonathan Amen, Regina Esposito,
	Gregg Glaviano, Judy Kirpich
client	Greenwell Goetz Architects
tools	Macromedia FreeHand, Quark XPress
paper/printing	French Frostone Frostbite and Tundra,
	Gilbert Neutech

design firm	Modelhart Grafik-Design DA
art director	Herbert O. Modelhart
designer	Herbert O. Modelhart
client	Optik Mayr
tools	Quark XPress, Adobe Illustrator, Adobe Photoshop
paper/printing	Olin/Two-color, Business Card Cellophane

326 Edwardia Dr./ Greensboro, NC 27409 / 336 854 8828 ph / 336 854 3713 fx / www.studioplace.com

StudioPlace

326 Edwardia Dr./ Greensboro, NC 27409

StudioPlace

KEVIN LEE
photographer

StudioPlace
326 Edwardia Dr.
Greensboro, NC 27409
336 854 8828 ph
336 854 3713 fx
www.studioplace.com

design firm	Henderson Tyner Art Co.
art director	Troy Tyner
designers	Troy Tyner, Amanda Love
client	Place Photography
tool	Macromedia FreeHand
paper/printing	Strathmore Writing/Dicksons Printing Co.

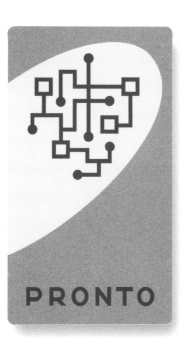

design firm	Korn Design
art director	Denise Korn
designer	Javier Cortés
client	Pronto Product Development
tools	Adobe Illustrator 7.0, Power Macintosh
paper/printing	Alpha Press

PRONTO PRODUCT DEVELOPMENT CORPORATION
22 Highland Terrace / Marblehead, MA 01945

PRONTO PRODUCT
DEVELOPMENT

David Moschella

22 Highland Terrace
Marblehead, MA 01945
dmoschella@prontoproduct.com

T : 781 / 631 1284
F : 781 / 631 4360

ABAecom

A subsidiary of the AMERICAN BANKERS ASSOCIATION

www.ABAecom.com   800·338·0626   1120 CONNECTICUT AVENUE, NW   WASHINGTON, DC 20036

design firm	**Focus Design & Marketing Solutions**
art director	**Aram Youssefian**
designer	**Aram Youssefian**
client	**Kogei, America**
tools	**Quark XPress 4.0, Adobe Illustrator 7.0, Adobe Photoshop 4.0**

ABAecom

1120 CONNECTICUT AVENUE, NW
WASHINGTON, DC 20036

ABAecom

www.ABAecom.com

202·663·5387 PHONE   202·828·4532 FAX
1120 CONNECTICUT AVENUE, NW · WASHINGTON, DC 20036

design firm	Woodworth Associates
art director	Brad Woodworth
designer	Steve Westfal
client	Landmark Builders
tools	Adobe Pagemaker, Macromedia FreeHand
paper/printing	Strathmore Writing/Offset

design firm	Karacters Design Group
creative director	Maria Kennedy
designer	Matthew Clark
client	Rick Etkin Photography
tools	Adobe Illustrator, Macintosh
paper/printing	Confetti/Broadway Printers

design firm	Greteman Group
art directors	Sonia Greteman, James Strange
designer	James Strange
client	Austin Miller
tools	Macintosh, Macromedia FreeHand

design firm	Seltzer Design
art director	Rochelle Seltzer
designer	Louise Magni
client	Career Investment Strategies, Inc.
tools	Quark XPress 3.32, Macintosh 8600 Power PC
paper/printing	Classic Crest/Two color

CAREER INVESTMENT
STRATEGIES, INC.

CAREER INVESTMENT
STRATEGIES, INC.

ONE STATE STREET, SUITE 950
BOSTON, MA 02109 USA

ONE STATE STREET, SUITE 950
BOSTON, MA 02109 USA
TEL 617 720 2244 • FAX 617 720 2644

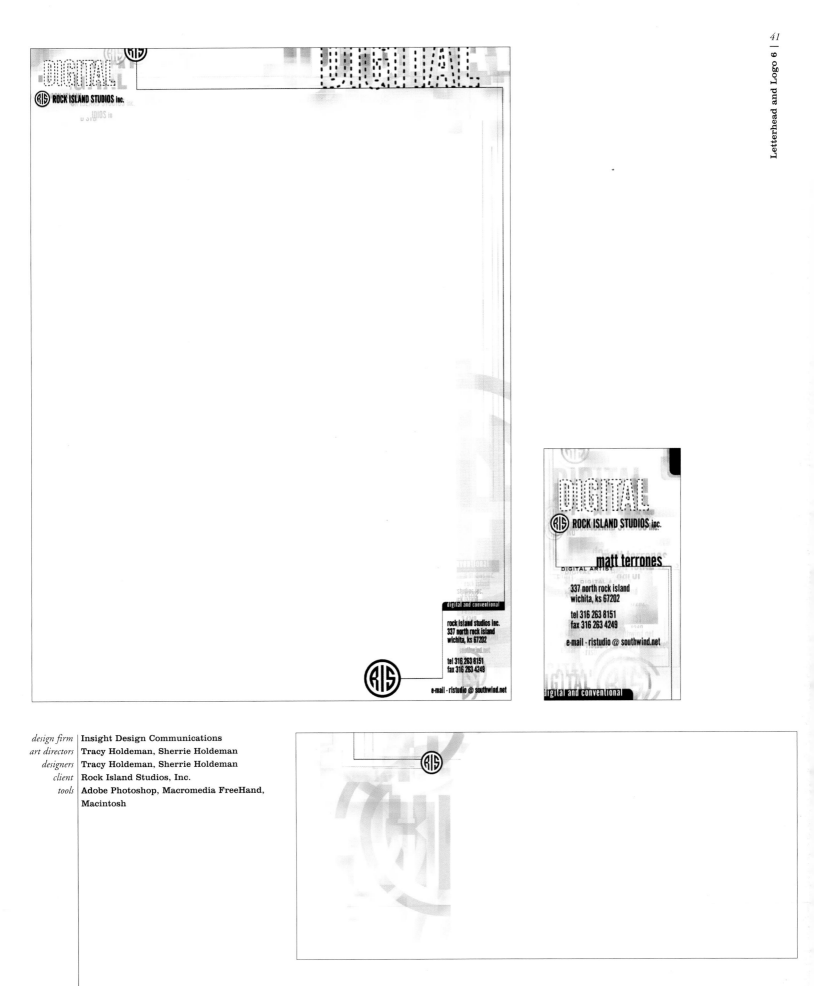

design firm | Insight Design Communications
art directors | Tracy Holdeman, Sherrie Holdeman
designers | Tracy Holdeman, Sherrie Holdeman
client | Rock Island Studios, Inc.
tools | Adobe Photoshop, Macromedia FreeHand,
Macintosh

VECTOR XXI,
Estudos de
Desenvolvimento
Económico e Social, Lda.

Av. Central, 45
Tel. 053. 616906/510
Fax 053. 611872
4710 Braga
Portugal

design firm	**Vestígio, Lda.**
art director	**Emanuel Barbosa**
designer	**Emanuel Barbosa**
client	**Vector XXI**
tools	**Macromedia FreeHand, Adobe Photoshop, Macintosh**

design firm	Nesnadny + Schwartz
designers	Mark Schwartz, Joyce Nesnadny
client	Fortran Printing, Inc.
tools	Quark XPress, Adobe Illustrator, Adobe Photoshop
paper/printing	70 lb. Champion Benefit Cream/Fortran Printing, Inc.

design firm	Warren Group
art director	Linda Warren
designer	Annette Hanzer Pfau
client	Candace Pearson
tools	Quark XPress, Adobe Illustrator
paper/printing	Strathmore Writing/Barbara's Place

(candace PEARSON) THE WRITERS' PROJECT : 2016 Valentine Street Los Angeles, CA 90026

213.665-0615 telephone

213.665-0990 facsimile

cp813@westworld.com

¹Halley's Comet.

²Indy 500. (THINGS THAT M O V E)

³San Andreas Fault.

⁴Candace Pearson.

CANDACE PEARSON IS PLEASED TO ANNOUNCE
she has moved to new offices.

Same phone numbers. Same great copywriting.

ADS. ANNUALS. COLLATERAL. DIRECT MAIL. PACKAGING. PRODUCT NAMING. WEB WORK.

(candace PEARSON)

213.665-0615 telephone

THE WRITERS' PROJECT

A   MODERN

213.665-0990 facsimile

2016 Valentine Street   cp813@westworld.com
Los Angeles, CA 90026

(candace PEARSON)   THE WRITERS' PROJECT
2016 Valentine Street
Los Angeles, CA 90026

A   MODERN

(candace PEARSON)
THE WRITERS' PROJECT
2016 Valentine Street Los Angeles, CA 90026

K A A A
SEMITIC GREEK ETRUSCAN LATIN MODERN

(DEVELOPMENT OF MAJUSCULE)
FIRST LETTER OF THE ENGLISH ALPHABET
developed from Greek alpha

design firm	**Never Boring Design Associates**
art director	**David Boring**
designer	**Alexander Hillmer**
client	**JCD Concept**
tools	**Adobe Illustrator, Macintosh**
paper/printing	**Two color**

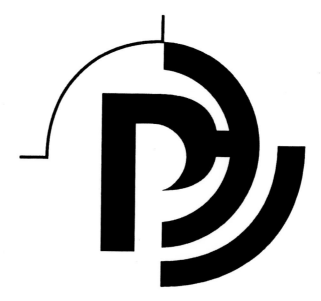

design firm | Fusion
art director | Barbara Chan
designer | Barbara Chan
client | Public Engineering Services, Inc.
tools | Adobe Illustrator 7.0, Macintosh G3

design firm | X Design Company
art director | Alex Valderrama
designer | Alex Valderrama
client | Rep File, Inc.

design firm	**Earthlink Creative Services**
art director	**Aram Youssefian**
designer	**Barbara Chan**
client	**Earthlink Creative Services**
tools	**Adobe Illustrator 7.0, Quark XPress 4.0, Macintosh G3**
paper/printing	**Fox River Select/Costello Brothers Lithographers**

Law Offices of
LANCE A. LICHTER

TEL
414 375-6868

FAX
414 375-6869

w62 n551 Washington Avenue Cedarburg, Wisconsin 53012

design firm | Becker Design
art director | Neil Becker
designer | Neil Becker
client | Lance A. Lichter
tool | Quark XPress

Law Offices of
LANCE A. LICHTER

TEL
414 375-6868

FAX
414 375-6869

w62 n551
Washington Avenue Cedarburg, Wisconsin
53012

Law Offices of
LANCE A. LICHTER

w62 n551 Washington Avenue Cedarburg, Wisconsin 53012

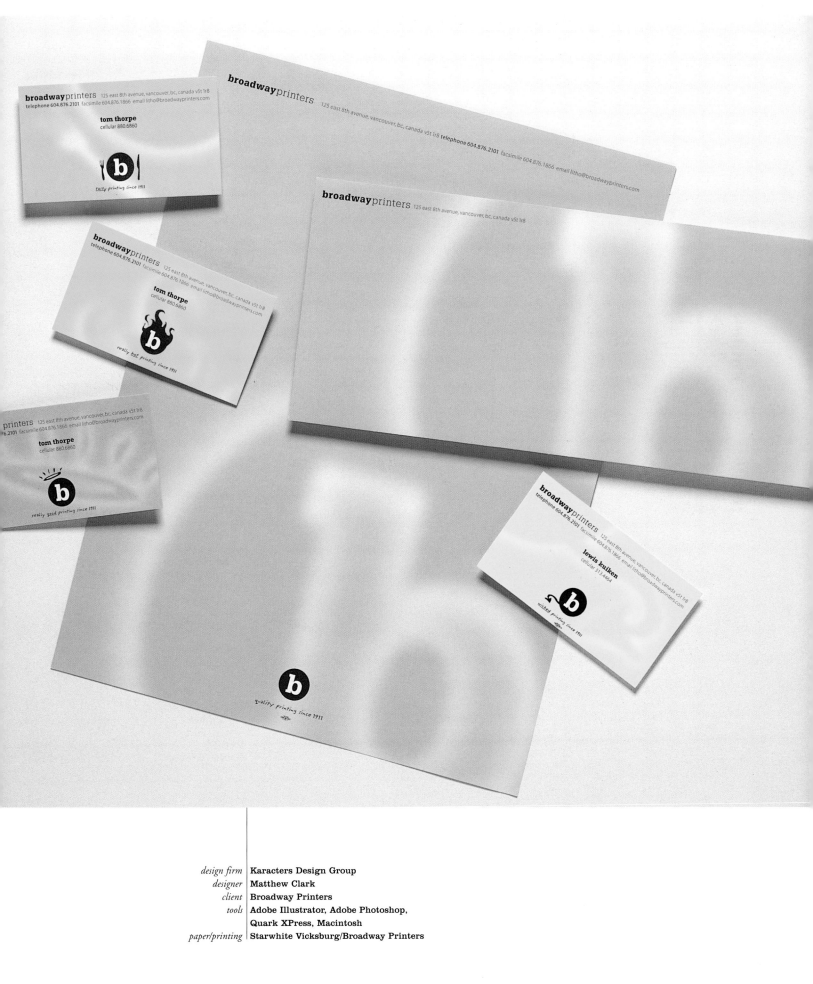

design firm | **Karacters Design Group**
designer | **Matthew Clark**
client | **Broadway Printers**
tools | **Adobe Illustrator, Adobe Photoshop,**
| **Quark XPress, Macintosh**
paper/printing | **Starwhite Vicksburg/Broadway Printers**

SPIN PRODUCTIONS TORONTO/ATLANTA WWW.SPINPRO.COM
620 KING ST WEST TORONTO ONTARIO CANADA M5V 1M6
TELEPHONE 416 504 8333 FACSIMILE 416 504 3876

SPIN PRODUCTIONS

KATHI PROSSER
ART DIRECTOR
kathi@spinpro.com

O ONTARIO CANADA M5V 1M6
416 504 8333 FACSIMILE 416 504 3876

620 KING STREET WEST TORONTO ONTARIO CANADA M5V 1M6
SPIN PRODUCTIONS
WWW.SPINPRO.COM TELEPHONE 416 504 8333

SPIN PRODUCTIONS TORONTO/ATLANTA WWW.SPINPRO.COM
620 KING ST WEST TORONTO ONTARIO CANADA M5V 1M6
TELEPHONE 416 504 8333 FACSIMILE 416 504 3876

SPIN PRODUCTIONS

DALE SMITH
CREATIVE DIRECTOR
dale@spinpro.com

SPIN PRODUCTIONS

design firm	Spin Productions
art directors	Dale Smith, Kathi Prosser
designers	Dale Smith, Kathi Prosser
client	Spin Productions
tools	Adobe Illustrator, Adobe Photoshop
paper/printing	Plainfield Pinweave/CJ Graphics

WALDY martens PHOTOGRAPHY
3rd floor, 291 east 2nd avenue
vancouver, british columbia, canada v5t 1b8
t [604]874-0002 f [604]874-2008

XXX
stimulating photography
RATING

XXX
stimulating photography
RATING

XXX

DO NOT BEND
RATING
WALDY martens PHOTOGRAPHY

XXX
stimulating photography
RATING

YOUR EYES ONLY
WALDY martens PHOTOGRAPHY
RATING

XXX
RATING
stimulating photography

WALDY martens PHOTOGRAPHY
3rd floor, 291 east 2nd avenue, vancouver, british columbia, canada v5t 1b8
t [604]874-0002 f [604]874-2008

3rd floor, 291 east 2nd avenue, vancouver, british columbia, canada v5t 1b8
WALDY martens PHOTOGRAPHY
t [604]874-0002 f [604]874-2008

design firm	Karacters Design Group
designer	Matthew Clark
client	Waldy Martens Photography
tools	Adobe Illustrator, Quark XPress, Adobe Photoshop, Macintosh
paper/printing	Domtar Naturals Kraft/Academy Press

professional services

SCOTT STOLL

PHOTOGRAPHY

5013 Pacific Highway East #20
Tacoma, Washington 98424
[253]896-0133

design firm	Belyea
art director	Patricia Belyea
designer	Christian Salas
client	Scott Stoll Photography
tools	Adobe Illustrator, Macintosh
paper/printing	Strathmore Writing Ultimate White

SCOTT STOLL

PHOTOGRAPHY

5013 Pacific Highway East #20
Tacoma, Washington 98424

design firm | **Big Eye Creative**
art directors | **Perry Chua, Nancy Yeasting**
designers | **Perry Chua, Nancy Yeasting**
client | **Clarke Printing**
tools | **Adobe Illustrator, Adobe Photoshop**
paper/printing | **Starwhite Vicksburg/Clarke Printing**

www.dwl.on.ca

Tel: 416 410 1729   Fax: 416 603 4731
202 Euclid Ave Toronto Ontario Canada M6J 2J9

design firm | **Russell, Inc.**
art director | **Laura Wills**
designer | **Laura Wills**
client | **DWL, Inc.**

design firm | Greteman Group
art directors | Sonia Greteman, James Strange
designer | James Strange
client | R. Messner
tools | Macromedia FreeHand, Macintosh

design firm | Barbara Chan Design
art director | Barbara Chan
designer | Barbara Chan
client | Husband & Associates
tools | Adobe Illustrator 7.0, Macintosh G3

design firm | Russell, Inc.
art director | Laura Wills
designer | Laura Wills
client | Certicom, Inc.

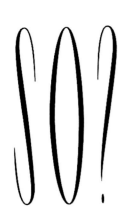

design firm	After Hours Creative
art director	After Hours Creative
designer	After Hours Creative
client	Second Opinion

design firm | **Siebert Design**
art director | **Lori Siebert**
client | **Scott Hull Associates**
paper/printing | **Arnold Printing**

design firm | Russell, Inc.
art director | Bob Russell
designer | Laura Wills
client | Radnet, Inc.

radnet

radnet inc. www.radnet.com
58 Charles Street, Cambridge
MA 02141-2147
T. 617.577.9422 F. 617.577.9377

radnet inc. www.radnet.com
58 Charles Street, Cambridge
MA 02141-2147
T. 617.577.9422 F. 617.577.9377
steve_hochschild@radnet.com

professional services

design firm	**Square One Design**
art director	**Lin Ver Menlen**
designer	**Lisa Vitalbo**
client	**Via**
tools	**Adobe Illustrator, Quark XPress, Power Tower 180**
paper/printing	**Strathmore Writing/D & D Printing Company**

via

Via Design Inc. 49 Monroe Center Grand Rapids, MI 49503 **Tel** 616.774.2022 **Fax** 616.774.4028 **E-mail** Via@ViaDesign-Inc.com

via

Via Design Inc. 49 Monroe Center Grand Rapids, MI 49503

via

via

...gn Inc. 49 Monroe Center Grand Rapids, MI 49503

TMG classic mini radios

design firm | Jim Lange Design
art director | Genji Leclair
designer | Jim Lange
client | TMG
tool | Macintosh

design firm | Synergy Design
art director | Leon Alvarado
designer | Leon Alvarado
client | The Room
tools | Macromedia FreeHand, Macintosh
paper/printing | Vinyl/Silk screening

design firm | Choplogic
art directors | Walter McCord, Mary Cawein
designers | Walter McCord, Mary Cawein
client | Internet Tool & Die
tools | Adobe Ilustrator, Quark XPress
paper/printing | Fox River, Simpson Starwhite Vicksburg/
| Two-color lithography

design firm | **X Design Company**
art director | **Alex Valderrama**
designer | **Alex Valderrama**
client | **Avrin Public Relations**

PROCESS SOLUTIONS

NEAL G. ANDERSON, PH.D.

129 UPPER CREEK ROAD, STOCKTON, NJ 08559
PHONE: (908) 996-2585, FAX: (908) 996-6505
E-MAIL: ANDERSON@ECLIPSE.NET

design firm | **Howard Levy Design**
art director | **Howard Levy**
designer | **Howard Levy**
client | **Process Solutions**

PROCESS SOLUTIONS

129 UPPER CREEK ROAD, STOCKTON, NJ 08559
PHONE: (908) 996-2585, FAX: (908) 996-6505
E-MAIL: ANDERSON@ECLIPSE.NET

design firm	Plum Notion Design Laboratory
art director	Damion Silver
designer	Damion Silver
client	Bikers Edge Bike Shop
tools	Adobe Illustrator, Adobe Photoshop

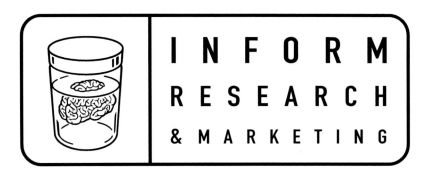

design firm	Han/Davis Group
art director	Ed Han
designer	Ed Han
client	Inform Research & Marketing
tool	Adobe Illustrator

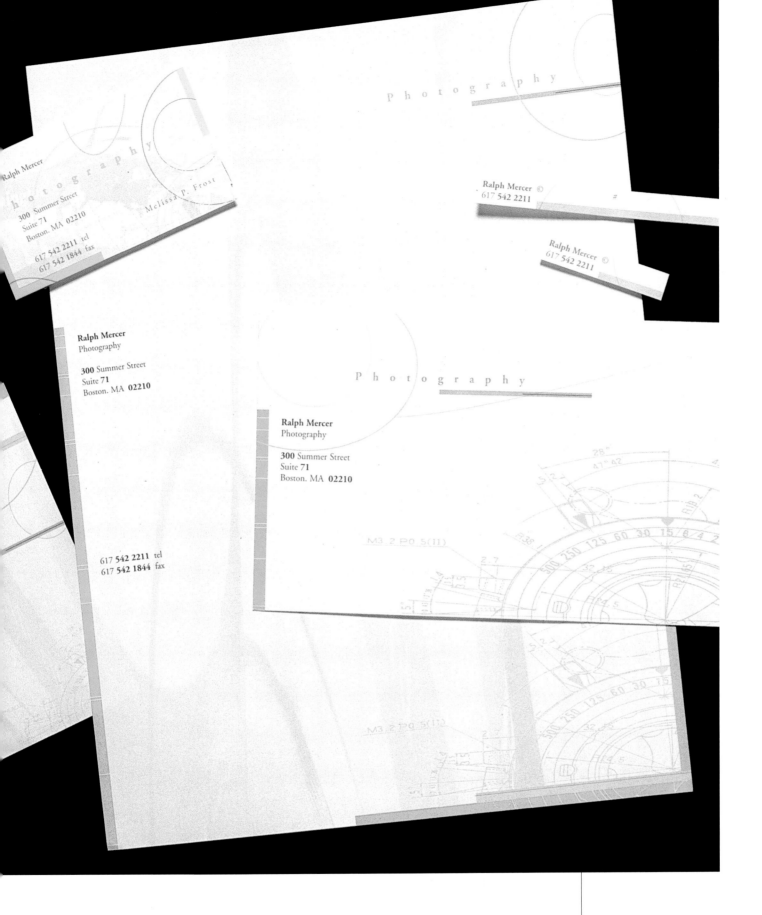

Ralph Mercer
Photography

300 Summer Street
Suite 71
Boston. MA 02210

617 542 2211 tel
617 542 1844 fax

Ralph Mercer
Photography

300 Summer Street
Suite 71
Boston. MA 02210

Ralph Mercer ©
617 542 2211

Ralph Mercer ©
617 542 2211

Photography

Photography

design firm	Laughlin/Winkler, Inc.
art directors	Mark Laughlin, Ellen Winkler
designer	Ellen Winkler
client	Ralph Mercer Photography
tools	Quark XPress, Macintosh G3
paper/printing	Mohawk/Alpha Press

design firm	Design Guys
art director	Steven Sikora
designer	Amy Kirkpatrick
client	Mike Rabe Music Engraving
tool	Adobe Illustrator
paper/printing	Gray Fine Art Paper, Beckett Concept Sand Text, Curtis Black Vellum Cover/Offset, Park Printing, Exceptional Engraving (Card)

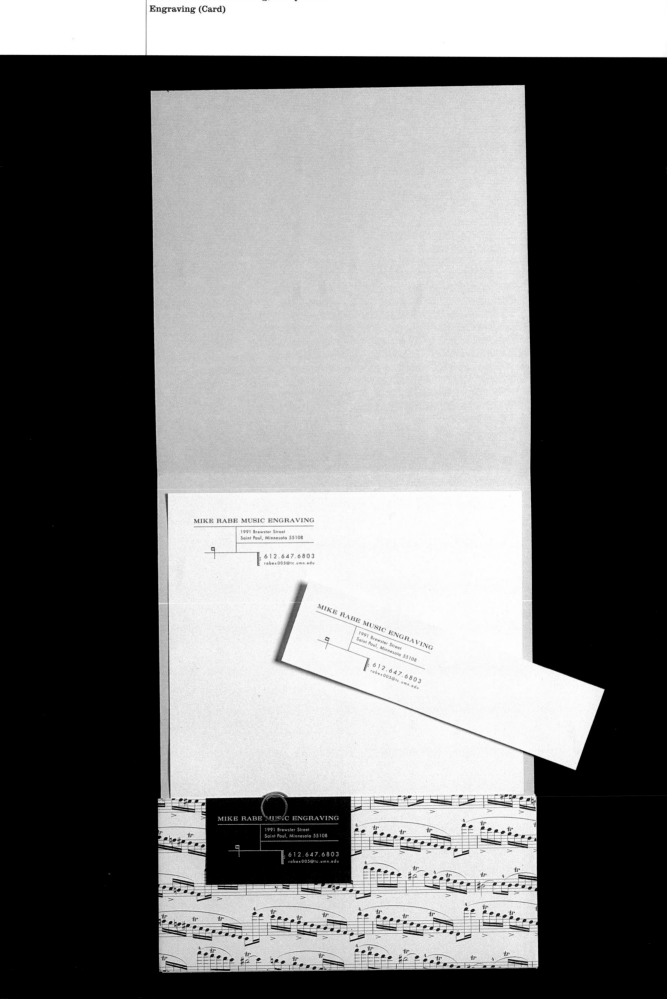

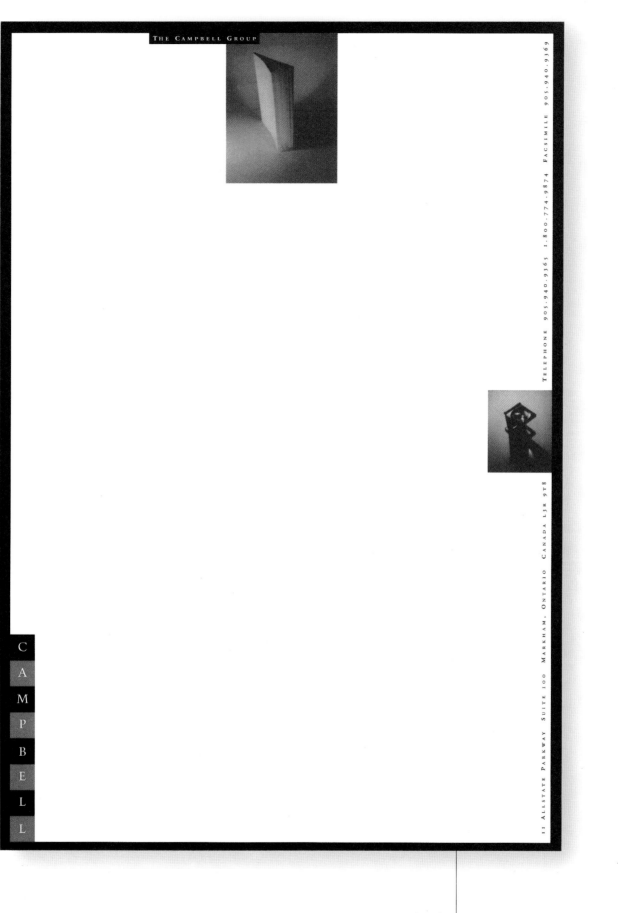

THE CAMPBELL GROUP

C
A
M
P
B
E
L
L

11 ALLSTATE PARKWAY SUITE 100 MARKHAM, ONTARIO CANADA L3R 9T8 TELEPHONE 905·940·9365 1·800·774·9874 FACSIMILE 905·940·9369

design firm	Vanderbyl Design
art director	Michael Vanderbyl
designer	Michael Vanderbyl
photographer	Michael Vanderbyl
client	The Campbell Group
tool	Quark XPress
paper/printing	Starwhite Vicksburg-The Campbell Group

design firm | **Hamagami/Carroll & Associates**
art director | **Justin Carroll**
designer | **Tony Mauro**
client | **Twentieth-Century Fox**

design firm | **Hamagami/Carroll & Associates**
art director | **Justin Carroll**
designer | **Tony Mauro**
client | **Twentieth-Century Fox**

design firm	Belyea
art director	Patricia Belyea
designer	Ron Lars Hansen
client	Belyea
tools	Adobe Illustrator, Macintosh
paper/printing	Strathmore/Artcraft

design firm | **Design Center**
art director | **John Reger**
designer | **Sherwin Schwartzrock**
client | **Benchmark QA**
tools | **FreeHand, Macintosh**

612 | 897.3505

BENCHMARK Q A

America's Software Quality Assurance Specialists

7600 Parklawn Avenue, Suite 408, Minneapolis, MN 55435

E-Mail | BenchmarkQA.com

Fax | 612.897.3524

designer	**Perry Chua**
client	**Metasoft Systems, Inc.**
tools	**Adobe Illustrator 6.0, Adobe Photoshop 4.0, Macintosh**
paper/printing	**Starwhite Vicksburg/Clarke Printing**

G E N E S I S   I N S T I T U T E

#3 PLAZA FRONTENAC   FRONTENAC, MO 63131.3507   314.432.1772 FAX 432.2265

design firm	**Bartels & Company**
art director	**David Bartels**
designer	**Ron Rodemacher**
client	**Genesis Institute**
tools	**Adobe Illustrator, Macintosh**
paper/printing	**Midwest Printing**

G E N E S I S

I N S T I T U T E

TIMOTHY JONES, MD

#3 PLAZA FRONTENAC

FRONTENAC, MO 63131.3507

314.432.1772 FAX 432.2265

design firm	Rupert Bassett
art directors	Rupert Bassett, Stuart Harvey Lee
designer	Rupert Bassett
client	Prime Studio
tools	Quark XPress, Macintosh Power PC
paper/printing	Mohawk Navajo/Offset lithography

Stuart Harvey Lee

Prime Studio
326 7th Avenue
3rd Floor
New York City
NY 10001

Telephone
212 967 0320

Fax
212 967 0743

E-mail
infoprime@
aol.com

Prime Studio
326 7th Avenue
3rd Floor
New York City
NY 10001

Prime Studio
326 7th Avenue
3rd Floor
New York City
NY 10001

Prime Studio
326 7th Avenue
3rd Floor
New York City
NY 10001

Telephone
212 967 0320

Fax
212 967 0743

E-mail
infoprime@
aol.com

visual dialogue

COLUMBUS AVE #1
BOSTON MASS 02116
(617) 247-3658 tel/fax
www.visualdialogue.com

MBUS AVENUE NUMBER 1 · BOSTON MASSACHUSE

AVE WO

GU

FOR A CREATIV SOLU

creative services

MILLER'S THUMB
BREWING COMPANY

RESTAURANT AND
MICROBREWERY

THE CANAL

Mo Templeton
General Manager

300 Bearsden Road   Anniesland   Glasgow G13 1EP
t: 0141 954 5333   f: 0141 954 5533
e: miller@millersthumb.com
w: www.millersthumb.com

10 Clairmont Gardens   Glasgow G3 7LW
t: 0141 331 7600   f: 0141 332 0336 · e: miller@millersthumb.com   w: www.millersthumb.com

design firm	**Teviot**
art directors	**Jane Hall, Kate Laing**
designer	**Jim Ramsay**
client	**Miller's Thumb Microbrewery**
tools	**Quark XPress, Adobe Illustrator 6.0**
paper/printing	**Metaphor Cream/Two-color spot lithography**

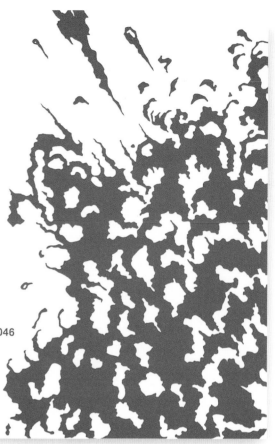

KIRIMA DESIGN Telephone 06-351-7045 Facsimile 06-351-7046

KIRIMA DESIGN Telephone 06-6351-7045 Facsimile 06-6351-7046

Yoriki-Cho Park-Bldg. 5F
1-5 Yoriki-Cho Kita-Ku Osaka-City
530-0036 Japan

キリマデザイン事務所
〒530-0036大阪市北区与力町1-5与力町パークビル5F

design firm | Kirima Design Office
art director | Harumi Kirima
designers | Harumi Kirima, Fumitaka Yukawa
client | Kirima Design Office

design firm	Shook Design Group
art director	Ginger Riley
designers	Steve Fenton, Dave Gibson
client	Walker Willhelm Productions
tools	Quark XPress, Adobe Photoshop, Macintosh G3
paper/printing	Classic Crest Solar White/Two-color offset

design firm	Knezic Parone Advertising
designers	Joe Knezic/Mike Parone/Robinson Smith
designer	Robinson Smith
client	WireHead Business Technologies
tool	Adobe Illustrator

design firm	Seltzer Design
art director	Rochelle Seltzer
designers	Rochelle Seltzer, Heather Roy
client	Seltzer Design
tools	Quark XPress 3.32, Adobe Illustrator 7.01, Macintosh 8600 Power PC
paper/printing	Astrolite/Two color (IPMS, ITOYO)

design firm | Hornall Anderson Design Works, Inc.
art director | Jack Anderson
designer | Mike Calkins
client | Hammerquist & Halverson
tool | Macromedia FreeHand
paper/printing | Mohawk, Navajo/Thermography on Business Card

Loja das Ideias

Rua do Campo Alegre, 1306
Salas 101, 102, 103 • 4150 Porto
Tel. 6069389/9402 • Fax 6097037
lojaideias@mail.telepac.pt
http://www.corimagem.pt/ideias/

design firm | **João Machado Design, Lda**
art director | **João Machado**
designer | **João Machado**
client | **Loja das Ideias**
tools | **Macromedia FreeHand, Quark XPress**
paper/printing | **Fedrigonni, Marcata 140 gsm**

Cor da Imagem

Rua do Viriato, 27 1ºB

1050 Lisboa

Tel. (01) 315 1527 • Fax (01) 355 6942

Rua do Campo Alegre, 1306

Sala 102 • 4150 Porto

Tel. (02) 609 5096 • Fax (02) 609 7037

covimagem@mail.telepac.pt

http://www.covimagem.pt

design firm	**João Machado Design, Lda**
art director	**João Machado**
designer	**João Machado**
client	**Côr da Imagem**
tools	**Macromedia FreeHand, Quark XPress**
paper/printing	**Fedrigonni, Marcata 140 gsm**

Cor da Imagem

Rua do Viriato, 27 1ºB • 1050 Lisboa

Rua do Campo Alegre, 1306 • Sala 102 • 4150 Porto

design firm	**João Machado Design, Lda**
art director	**João Machado**
designer	**João Machado**
client	**Ideias Virtuais**
tools	**Macromedia FreeHand, Quark XPress**
paper/printing	**Fedrigonni, Marcata 140 gsm**

design firm	Henderson Tyner Art Co.
art directors	Troy Tyner, Hayes Henderson
designer	Troy Tyner
client	Henderson Tyner Art Co.
tool	Macromedia Freehand
paper/printing	Gilbert Oxford/Dicksons Printing Co.

design firm	Steven Curtis Design, Inc.
art director	Steve Curtis
designer	Steve Curtis
client	Steven Curtis Design, Inc.
tools	Quark XPress 4.0, Adobe Photoshop 5.0, Macintosh
paper/printing	Strathmore Writing, Ultra White Wove/ Anderson Printing

design firm	Plum Notion Design Laboratory
art director	Damion Silver
designer	Damion Silver
client	Plum Notion Design Laboratory

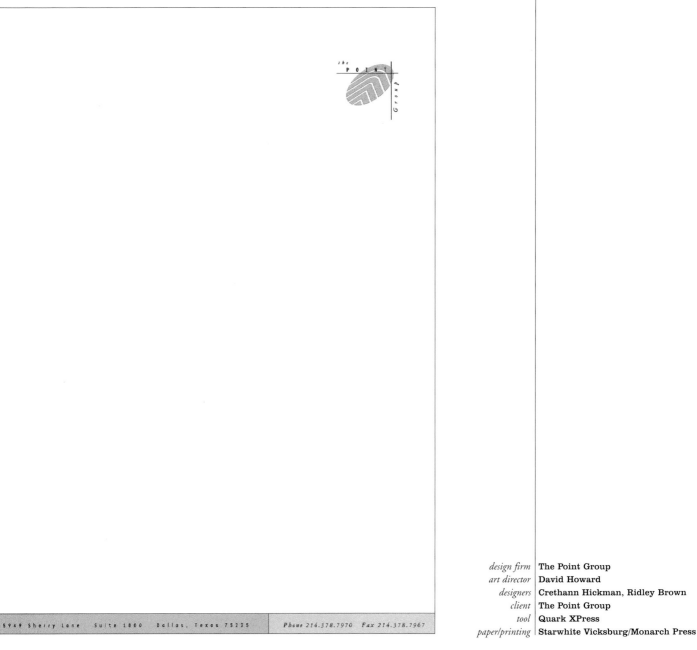

5949 Sherry Lane   Suite 1800   Dallas, Texas 75225   *Phone* 214.378.7970   *Fax* 214.378.7967

design firm	**The Point Group**
art director	**David Howard**
designers	**Crethann Hickman, Ridley Brown**
client	**The Point Group**
tool	**Quark XPress**
paper/printing	**Starwhite Vicksburg/Monarch Press**

design firm	Gouthier Design, Inc.
art director	Jonathan Gouthier
designer	Jonathan Gouthier
client	Gouthier Design, Inc.
tools	Quark XPress, Macintosh Quadra
paper/printing	Neenah Classic Crest Solar White/Joanne Miner

design firm	**Studio Hill**
art director	**Sandy Hill**
designers	**Sandy Hill, Alan Shimato**
client	**Studio Hill**
tools	**Quark XPress, Macintosh**
paper/printing	**70 lb. Mohawk Superfine Ultrawhite Eggshell Text**
	and 100 lb. Cover/Cottonwood Printing Co.

design firm | **Designstudio CAW**
designer | **Carsten-Andres Werner**
client | **Self-promotion**

DESIGNSTUDIO CAW

Carsten-Andres Werner | diplom grafikdesigner
Krugstraße 16 | 30453 Hannover | tel 0511.485.0295 | fax 0511.485.0299 |

kommunikationsgestaltung
mail@designstudio-caw.de

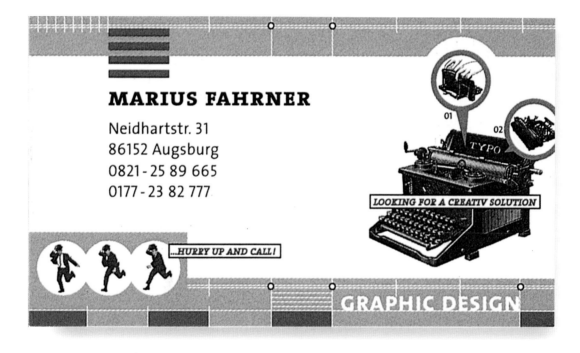

design firm	**Marius Fahrner**
art director	**Marius Fahrner**
designer	**Marius Fahrner**
client	**Self-promotion**
tool	**Macromedia FreeHand**
paper/printing	**Ròmerturm Countryside/Reset Hamburg**

design firm	Henderson Tyner Art Co.
art director	Troy Tyner
designer	Troy Tyner
client	Pam Fish
tool	Macromedia FreeHand
paper/printing	Strathmore Elements Grid/Topline Printing

mcg architecture

design firm	Selbert Perkins Design Collaborative
art director	Clifford Selbert
designers	Michelle Summers, Erin Miller
client	MCG Architects

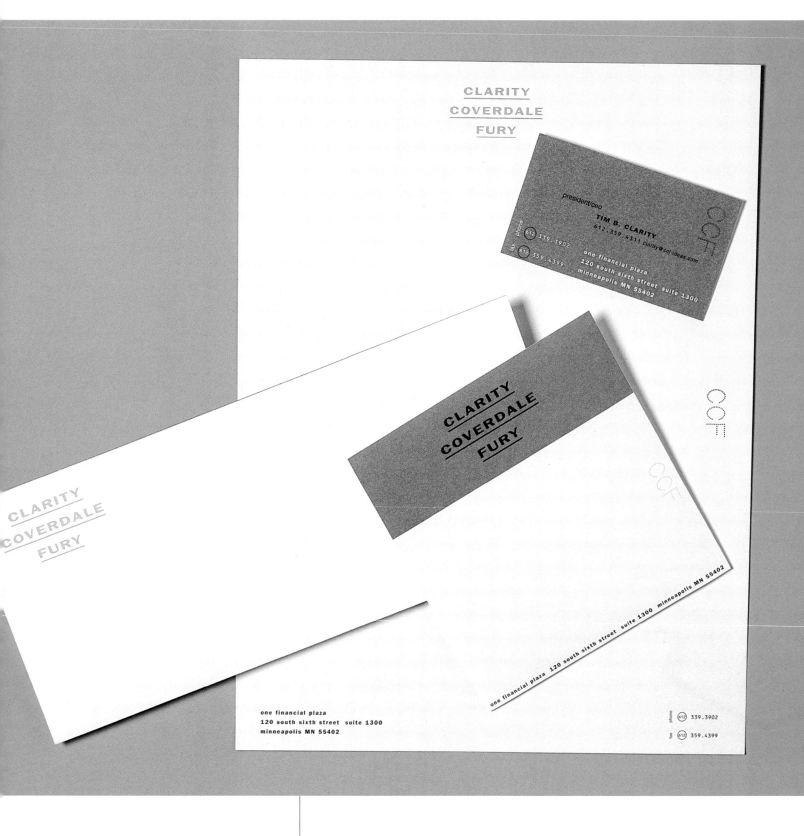

design firm	Parachute Design
designer	Cari Johnson
client	Clarity Coverdale Fury Advertising
tools	Quark XPress, Macintosh Power PC
paper/printing	Mohawk Superfine/Offset with Lazer Cutting on Detail

design firm	**Blue i Design**
art director	**Hellen Rayner**
designer	**Hellen Rayner**
client	**Blue i Design**
tools	**Quark XPress, Macromedia FreeHand, Macintosh**
paper/printing	**James River Classic Super Wove/ Cotswold Printing**

BLUE i DESIGN

Imperial House
Lypiatt Road
Cheltenham
Gloucestershire
GL50 2QJ
Telephone: 01242 234500
Fax: 01242 253360
ISDN: 01242 221587
email: info@bluei.co.uk

Blue i Design Limited
Registered Office:
Roberts House
2 Manor Road Ruislip
Middlesex
Registered in England
No. 3437151

sayegh design

24734 independence dr. #3111 . farmington hills, mi 48335 . phone/fax 248.442.9416 . email jsayegh1@flash.net

janelle sayegh . graphic designer

design firm	Sayegh Design
art director	Janelle Sayegh
designer	Janelle Sayegh
client	Sayegh Design
tools	Adobe Photoshop, Quark XPress, Macintosh
paper/printing	Neenah Classic Crest/Two color, Locke Printing Company

janelle sayegh . graphic designer

24734 independence dr. #3111 . farmington hills, mi 48335 . phone/fax 248.442.9416 . email jsayegh1@flash.net

design firm	what!design
art directors	Damon Meibers, Amy Strauch
designers	Damon Meibers, Amy Strauch
client	What!design
tool	Quark XPress
paper/printing	Ampad Engineer's Pad, Charrette Graph Paper, Oxford Card Guides/Laser, Stamp Pad, Wood Cut Stamp Rubber Type, Embosser

no.012

estimate

what!design
15 park vale street
brookline   ma 02446
fax 731 - 8916
617 738 - what [9428]

...08 issue for the January 1999 issue:
...ut and production

studio fees
pricing based on
28-page, 8.5" x ...

letter   01.26.99

what!design
15 park vale street
brookline   ma 02446
fax 731 - 8916
617 738 - what [9428]

image ma...
(based on
on 135 s...

date
01.26.99
client
X Corporation
project
X Corporation magazine
January 1999 issue

This estimate covers studio fees
and production costs to develop
and produce the following items:

studio fees
1) layout and production
client contact and me...
3) all costs for makin...

This estimate does...
following items:
2) original art (p...
illustration) 3) ...
and delivery ...

All projects ...
on acceptan...
...lf o...
t...

cover a...

interio...
price...
total...

what!design
15 park vale street
brookline   ma 02446

what!design
15 park vale street
brookline   ma 02446

DAMON MEIBERS
creative director
damonwhat @ world.std.com

?!

?!

?!

Regarding all of our...
with absolute accur...
exact number of p...
be billed at a pro...
30. 5. All agenc...
Client request o...
Mass Sales tax...

Mr. So-and-so
X Corporation
123 Long Drive
Reveah, MA 02061

ARROWSTREET GRAPHIC DESIGN

ARROWSTREET
GRAPHIC
DESIGN

Arrowstreet Inc
212 Elm Street
Somerville MA 02144
617.623.5555 fax 625.4646

**Michele Phelan
Assistant Director**

phelan@arrowstreet.com

ARROWSTREET GRAPHIC DESIGN
Arrowstreet Inc 212 Elm Street Somerville MA 02144

design firm	**Arrowstreet Graphic Design**
art directors	**Bob Lowe, Michele Phalen**
designer	**Trip Boswell**
client	**Arrowstreet Graphic Design**
tools	**Adobe Illustrator, Macintosh Power PC**
paper/printing	**Astrolite Smooth/United Lithograph**

design firm	Pham Phu Design
art director	Oanh Pham Phu
designer	Renald Strobel
client	Riesle Technological Consultants
paper/printing	Two color

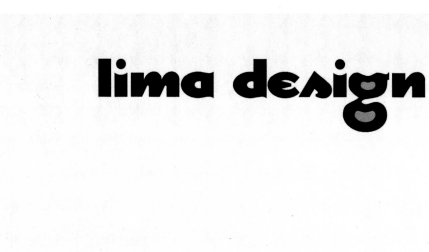

215 HANOVER STREET
BOSTON, MASSACHUSETTS 02113
617-FOR-BEAN [367-2326]
617-367-1255 [FAX]
BEANS@LIMADESIGN.COM
WWW.LIMADESIGN.COM

design firm	Lima Design
designers	Lisa McKenna, Mary Kiene
client	Lima Design
tools	Quark XPress, Macromedia FreeHand
paper/printing	Monadnock Caress/Shawmut Printing

PARDON OUR DUST
MCGAUGHY DESIGN
IS UNDERGOING RENOVATION

WE CAN STILL BE REACHED AT:
3706-A STEPPES COURT
FALLS CHURCH, VA 22041
703•578•1375 / FAX 578•9658
MCGDESIGN@AOL.COM

WE CAN STILL BE REACHED AT:
3706-A STEPPES COURT
FALLS CHURCH, VA 22041
703•578•1375 / FAX 578•9658
MCGDESIGN@AOL.COM

PARDON OUR DUST
MCGAUGHY DESIGN
IS UNDERGOING RENOVATION

WE CAN STILL BE REACHED AT:
3706-A STEPPES COURT
FALLS CHURCH, VA 22041
703•578•1375 / FAX 578•9658
MCGDESIGN@AOL.COM

design firm	McGaughy Design
art director	Malcolm McGaughy
designer	Malcolm McGaughy
client	McGaughy Design
tools	Macromedia FreeHand, Macintosh Power PC
paper/printing	Various/Rubber stamp

BIGBEATGROUP

10 clairmont gardens   glasgow G3 7LW

TEL 0141 **331 7600**
FAX 0141 332 0336
E-MAIL big_beat@compuserve.com

printed on recycled paper

big beat group limited   registered in scotland no 137725

design firm	Scott Stern
art director	Jonathan Frewin
designer	Jonathan Frewin
client	Big Beat Group Holdings Ltd
tool	Adobe Photoshop
paper/printing	Four-color process, spot color, Spot UV varnish

design firm	Visual Dialogue
art director	Fritz Klaetke
designers	Fritz Klaetke, Chris Reese
client	Visual Dialogue
tools	Quark XPress, Adobe Photoshop, Macintosh Power PC
paper/printing	Certificate Stock, Starwhite Vicksburg/Innerer
	Klang Press, Alpha Press

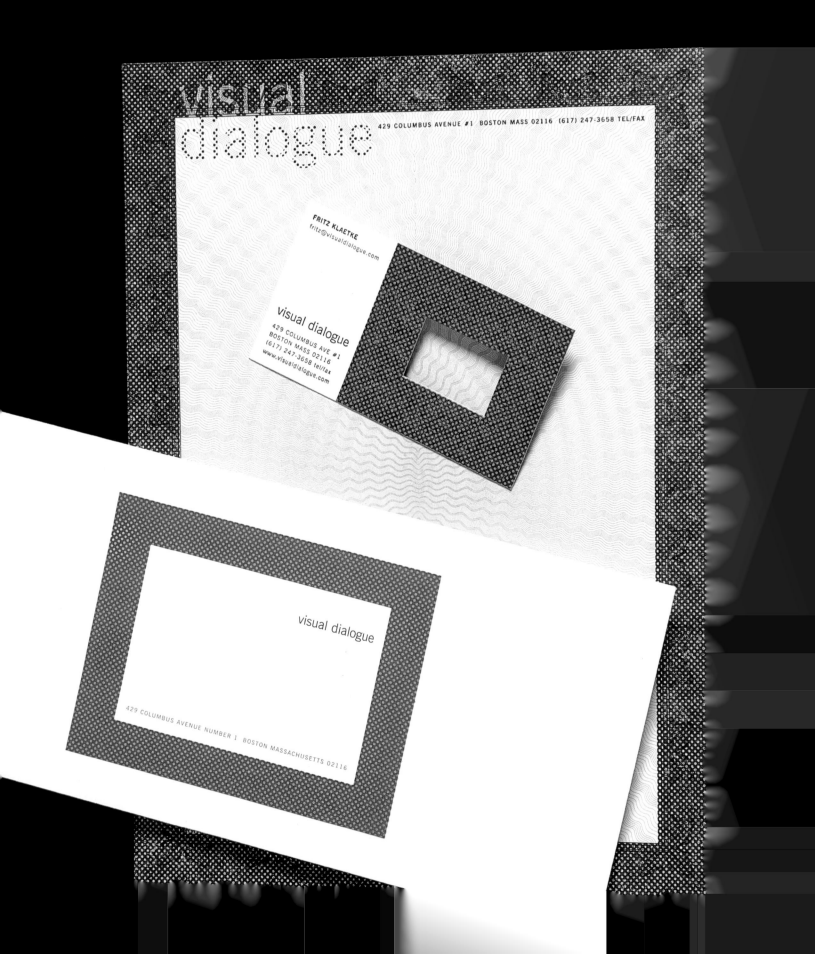

G3 Marketing und Kommunikation
Dr. Bernd Gschwandtner
Dr. Adolf-Altmann-Str. 17
A-5020 Salzburg

T +43-662-832601-0
F +43-662-832601-13
E g3-marketing@salzburg.co.at

design firm	Modelhart Grafik-Design DA
art director	Herbert O. Modelhart
designer	Herbert O. Modelhart
client	G3 Marketing und Kommunikation
tools	Quark XPress, Adobe Illustrator
paper/printing	118 lb. Strathmore Writing/Two color

design firm	Lux Design
art director	Amy Gregg
designer	Laura Cary
client	Good Dog Design
tools	Adobe Illustrator, Macintosh 9600/300 Power PC
paper/printing	Starwhite Vicksburg/R.W. Nielsen Associates

design firm	Focus Design & Marketing Solutions
art director	Aram Youssefian
designer	Aram Youssefian
client	Focus
tools	Adobe Illustrator 7.0, Adobe Photoshop 4.0, Macintosh G3
paper/printing	Strathmore Writing System/Lithographix

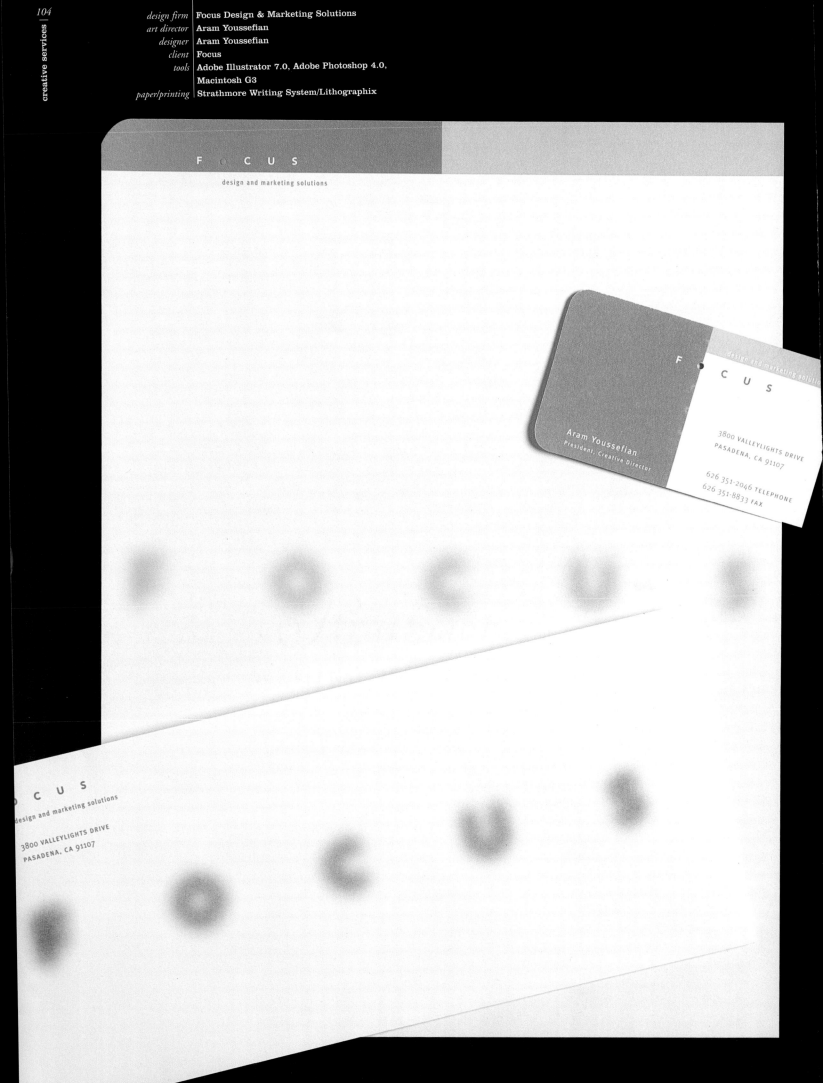

THE SOURCE OF THE FINEST
ARTISTS AND THEIR WORK

■■
931 EAST MAIN STREET ■ SUITE 3 ■ MADISON ■ WI ■ 53703
PHONE 608.257.2590 ■ FAX 608.257.2690 ■ WWW.GUILD.COM
■■

design firm	Planet Design Company
art director	Dana Lytle
designer	Ben Hirby
client	Guild.com
tools	Adobe Illustrator, Quark XPress
paper/printing	Neenah Classic Crest Natural White/
	American Printing

THE SOURCE OF THE FINEST
ARTISTS AND THEIR WORK

TONI SIKES
PRESIDENT

■■

TSIKES@GUILD.COM
931 E. MAIN ST. ■ STE. 3
MADISON ■ WI ■ 53703
PHONE ■ 608.257.2590
FAX ■ 608.257.2690

■■

design firm	Planet Design Company
art director	Kevin Wade
designer	Dan Ibarra
client	Brave World Productions
tools	Adobe Photoshop, Adobe Illustrator, Quark XPress
paper/printing	Mohawk Vellum Warm White/ American Printing

www.cuy2k.com | CREDIT UNION YEAR 2000

1464-P1042A

design firm	**Planet Design Company**
art director	**Kevin Wade**
designer	**Martha Graettinger**
client	**CUNA**
tools	**Adobe Illustrator, Quark XPress**
paper/printing	**Classic Crest Ultra White/Lithography Productions**

SALISBURY STUDIOS

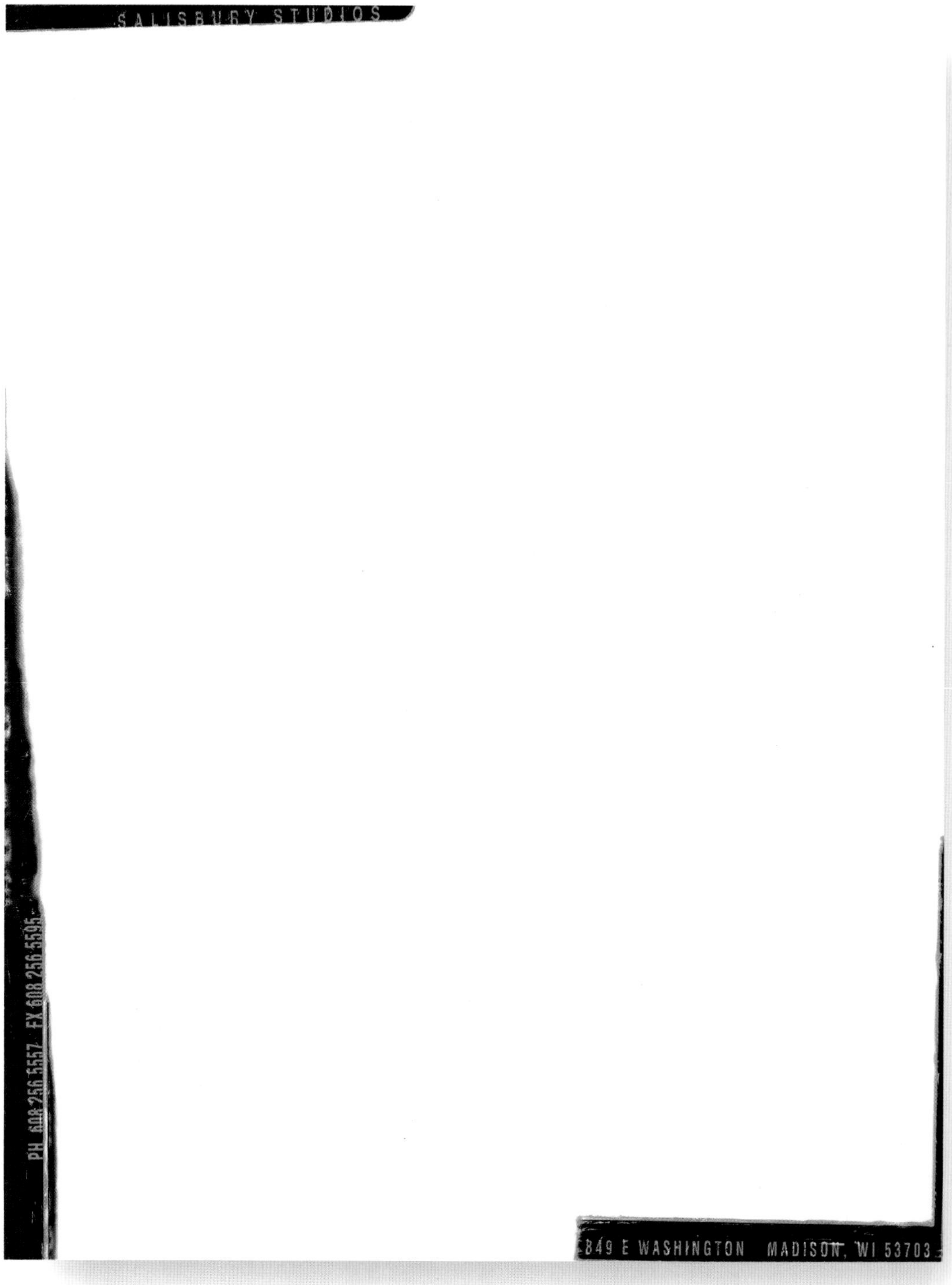

SALISBURY STUDIOS

design firm	Planet Design Company
art directors	Dana Lytle, Kevin Wade
designer	Raelene Mercer
client	Salisbury Studios
tools	Quark XPress, Adobe Photoshop

PH 608 256 5557 FX 608 256 5595

849 E WASHINGTON   MADISON, WI 53703

design firm	Modelhart Grafik-Design DA
art director	Herbert O. Modelhart
designer	Herbert O. Modelhart
client	Herbert O. Modelhart Grafik-Design
tool	Quark XPress
paper/printing	Strathmore Writing 118 gsm and 298 gsm/Two color

design firm | Lux Design
art director | Amy Gregg
designer | Amy Gregg
client | Lux Design
tools | Adobe Illustrator, Macintosh 9600/300 Power PC
paper/printing | Starwhite Vicksburg/Express Quality
Printing & Lasercraft

design firm	Hornall Anderson Design Works, Inc.
art director	Jack Anderson
designers	Jack Anderson, David Bates
client	Hornall Anderson Design Works, Inc.
tool	Macromedia FreeHand
paper/printing	French Durotone, Packing Grey Liner; French Durotone, Newsprint White

design firm	**Vestígio, Lda.**
art director	**Emanuel Barbosa**
designer	**Emanuel Barbosa**
client	**Vestígo**
tools	**Macromedia FreeHand, Macintosh 8100 Power PC**
paper/printing	**Favini/Two color**

Vestígio: *Consultores de Design, Lda.*
Edifício Hoechst, Av. Sidónio Pais, 379, Salas 4-5
P-4100 Porto, Portugal
Tel. *02. 6064117* **Fax** *02. 6064117*

V:

design firm | **Roslyn Eskind Associates Limited**
art director | **Roslyn Eskind**
designer | **Roslyn Eskind**
client | **Roslyn Eskind Associates Limited**
tools | **Quark XPress, Adobe Photoshop, Adobe Illustrator, Macintosh**
paper/printing | **Chartham/Seaway Printing**

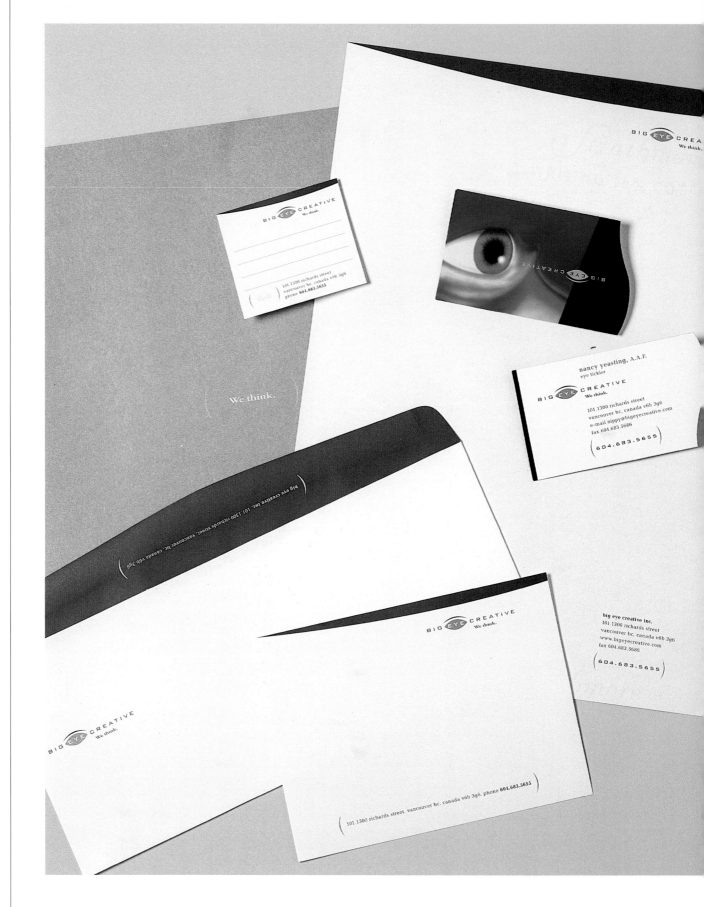

design firm	Big Eye Creative, Inc.
art director	Perry Chua
designer	Perry Chua
client	Big Eye Creative, Inc.
tools	Adobe Illustrator 6.0, Adobe Photoshop 4.0, Macintosh
paper/printing	Cards: 120 lb. McCoy, Rest: Strathmore Writing/Clarke Printing

RICHARDS ● DESIGN GROUP INC

5616 Kingston Pike, Suite 105
Knoxville, Tennessee 37919-6325

Post Office Box 10773
Knoxville, Tennessee 37939-0773

423-588-9707 Telephone
423-584-7741 Facsimile

www.richardsdesign.com

design firm	**Richards Design Group, Inc.**
art director	**Michael Richards**
designer	**Timothy D. Jenkins**
client	**Richards Design Group**
tools	**Adobe Illustrator, Quark XPress**
paper/printing	**Strathmore Soft White Wove/Ullrich Printing**

design firm	Visual Dialogue
art director	Fritz Klaetke
designer	Fritz Klaetke
client	Edana Reps
tools	Quark XPress, Adobe Photoshop, Macintosh Power PC
paper/printing	Strathmore Writing & Labor Stock/Alpha Press

design firm	**Karacters Design Group**
creative director	**Maria Kennedy**
designer	**Matthew Clark**
client	**Karacters Design Group**
tools	**Adobe Illustrator, Quark XPress,**
	Adobe Photoshop, Macintosh
paper/printing	**Classic Crest/Hemlock Printing**

karacters design group

karacters design group

1600 : 777 hornby street
vancouver, british columbia
canada v6z 2t3
telephone 604.640.4327
facsimile 604.640.4344

karacters design group

Twenty-five
Corporate Dr
Suite 218
Burlington
MA 01803

Phone 781·
273·2999

Fax 781·
273·3733

www.exhibit-a.com
eac@exhibit-a.com

design firm	**Exhibit A Communications**
art director	**Mark Gedrich**
designer	**Mark Gedrich**
client	**Exhibit A Communications**
tools	**Adobe Illustrator, Macintosh 9500 Power PC**

design firm	Burn World-Wide, Ltd.
art director	David L. Clarke
designer	Burn Staff
client	Burn World-Wide, Ltd.
tools	Adobe Illustrator, Adobe Photoshop
paper/printing	Classic Columns Stucco 80lb. text
	Haff and Duagherty, Miami, FL

digital image magic

2 Magnolia Avenue
San Anselmo Ca 94960

phone 415 453 2828
fax   415 453 0828
e-mail mailalightrain.com

design firm	**be**
art director	**William Burke**
designers	**Eric Read, Coralie Russo**
client	**Light Rain**
tools	**Adobe Photoshop, Adobe Illustrator**

ANNI KUAN

242 W 38TH ST NEW YORK NY 10018 PHONE 212 704 4038 FAX 704 0651

design firm	Sagmeister Inc.
art director	Stefan Sagmeister
designers	Stefan Sagmeister/Hjalti Karlsson
client	Anni Kuan Design
tools	Adobe Illustrator/Macintosh 9500 Power PC
paper/printing	Strathmore Writing/ Offset, Laser Die-Cut

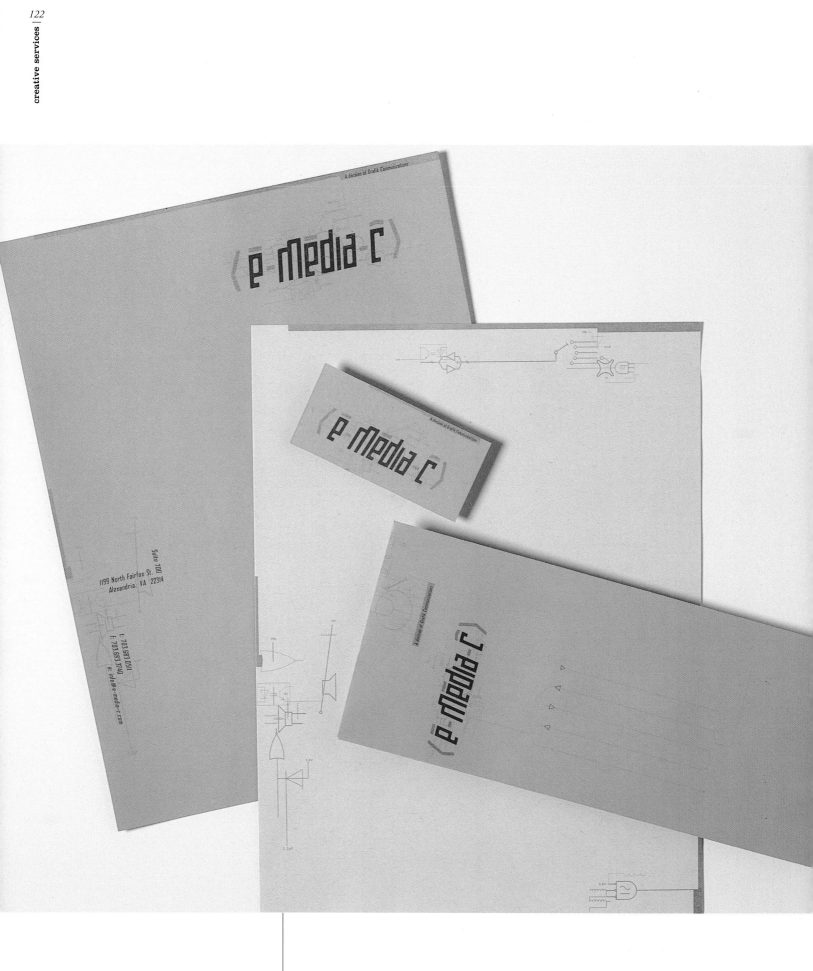

design firm	Grafik Communications, Ltd.
design team	Jonathan Amen, Eric Goetz
illustrator	Jonathan Amen
client	E-Media-C
tools	Macromedia FreeHand, Quark XPress
paper/printing	French Construction Fuse Green & Cement Green

MIRIELLO

GRAFICO

Graphic Communication

419 WEST G STREET, SAN DIEGO, CALIFORNIA 92101, 619 234-1124 · FAX 619 234-1960
VIA DALMAZIA, 4-31044 MONTEBELLUNA (TREVISO) ITALY, 0423/680310 (R.A.) FAX 0423/303365

design firm | **Miriello Grafico, Inc.**
art director | **Ron Miriello**
designer | **Ron Miriello**
client | **Miriello Grafico, Inc.**
tools | **Adobe Illustrator, Adobe Photoshop, Macintosh**
paper/printing | **Gilbert Esse/Offset litho four-color over**
| **two-color, hand-perforated edging, embossed**

MIRIELLO

GRAFICO, INC.

Graphic Communication

design firm | Elixir Design, Inc.
art director | Jennifer Jerde
designer | Michael Braley
client | Premier
tool | Adobe Illustrator

design firm | Mires Design
art director | Scott Mires
designer | Miguel Perez
illustrator | Miguel Perez
client | Jabra Corporation

JONELLE WEAVER

STUDIO
66 CROSBY #5D NEW YORK NEW YORK 10012
PHONE AND FAX 800·915·9331

OFFICE
268 HENRY STREET #2F BROOKLYN HEIGHTS NEW YORK 11201
PHONE AND FAX 800·915·9331

design firm	Elixir Design, Inc.
art director	Jennifer Jerde
designer	Jennifer Tolo
client	Jonelle Weaver
tools	Quark XPress, Adobe Illustrator
paper/printing	Scallop-edged placement stock

retail, restaurant, and hospitaliy

5850

Ellsworth

Avenue

Pittsburgh

Pennsylvania

15232

design firm | **Brabender Cox**
art director | **Stephen Smith**
designer | **Stephen Smith**
client | **ICON/Sports rock entertainment**
tool | **Adobe Illustrator**

design firm	Hornall Anderson Design Works, Inc.
art director	Hornall Anderson Design Works, Inc.
designers	Larry Anderson, Mary Hermes,
	Mike Calkins, Michael Brugman
client	U.S. Cigar
tools	Macromedia FreeHand

design firm | Barbara Chan Design
art director | Barbara Chan
designer | Barbara Chan
client | Recess
tools | Adobe Illustrator 7.0, Macintosh G3

design firm | Kirima Design Office
art director | Harumi Kirima
designer | Harumi Kirima
client | Happy-En

design firm | Jim Lange Design
art director | Lee Langill
designer | Jim Lange
client | Lee Langill
tool | Macintosh

design firm | Murrie Lienhart Rysner
art director | Linda Voll
designer | Linda Voll
client | Wellness Business Works
tool | Adobe Illustrator

design firm	Teviot
art director	Kate Laing
designer	Jim Ramsay
client	Teviot
tools	Quark XPress, Adobe Illustrator 6.0
paper/printing	Arjo Wiggins Hi-Five-Cyber/One-color lithography

TEVIOT

WITH COMPLIMENTS

TEVI

senior designer

T 0131 538 8307

JIM RAMSAY

TEVIOT

7 Dublin Street Lane South | Edinburgh EH1 3PX | T 0131 538 8300
F 0131 538 8330 | E teviot@teviot.co.uk | www.teviot.co.uk

7 Dublin Street Lane South | Edinburgh EH1 3PX | T 0131 538 8300 | F 0131 538 8330 | E teviot@teviot.co.uk | www.teviot.co.uk
26 Newton Place | Glasgow G3 7PY | T 0141 561 2221 | F 0141 564 1351
Associate Company: Biggart Porter Consultancy | part of Customer Relationship Management International LLC
Registered in Edinburgh as Teviot Design Limited No 161928

J. MELVILLE ENGLE
PRESIDENT,
CHIEF EXECUTIVE OFFICER

TEL: 781.932.6616
EXT. 106

ANIKA THERAPEUTICS, INC.
236 WEST CUMMINGS PARK
WOBURN, MA 01801

FAX: 781.932.3360
E-MAIL: MENGLE@
ANIKATHERAPEUTICS.COM

design firm	**Ellis Pratt Design, Inc.**
art director	**Vernon Ellis**
designer	**Elaine Pratt**
client	**Anika Therapeutics, Inc.**
tools	**Adobe Illustrator, Macintosh G3**
paper/printing	**Strathmore Writing/Maran Printing**

393 *Totten Pond Road*
Waltham, MA 02451
(781)487-9996 *direct*
(781)487-9997 *fax*
(877)363-9463 *gift orders*
SENDWINE.COM *website*

design firm | **Phillips Design Group**
art director | **Steve Phillips**
designers | **Alison Goudreault, Susan Logher**
client | **Sendwine.com**
tools | **Adobe Illustrator 7.0, Macintosh G3**
paper/printing | **Strathmore Writing, Soft White/**
| **BHF Printing**

MIKE LANNON
President & Founder

393 *Totten Pond Road*
Waltham, MA 02451
(781)487-9996 *direct*
(781)487-9997 *fax*
(877)363-9463 *gift orders*
MIKE@SENDWINE.COM

design firm	Arrowstreet Graphic Design
art director	Bob Lowe
designer	Seth Londergan
client	Pet Corner, LLC
tools	Adobe Illustrator, Macintosh Power PC
paper/printing	Poseidon White/Direct Printing

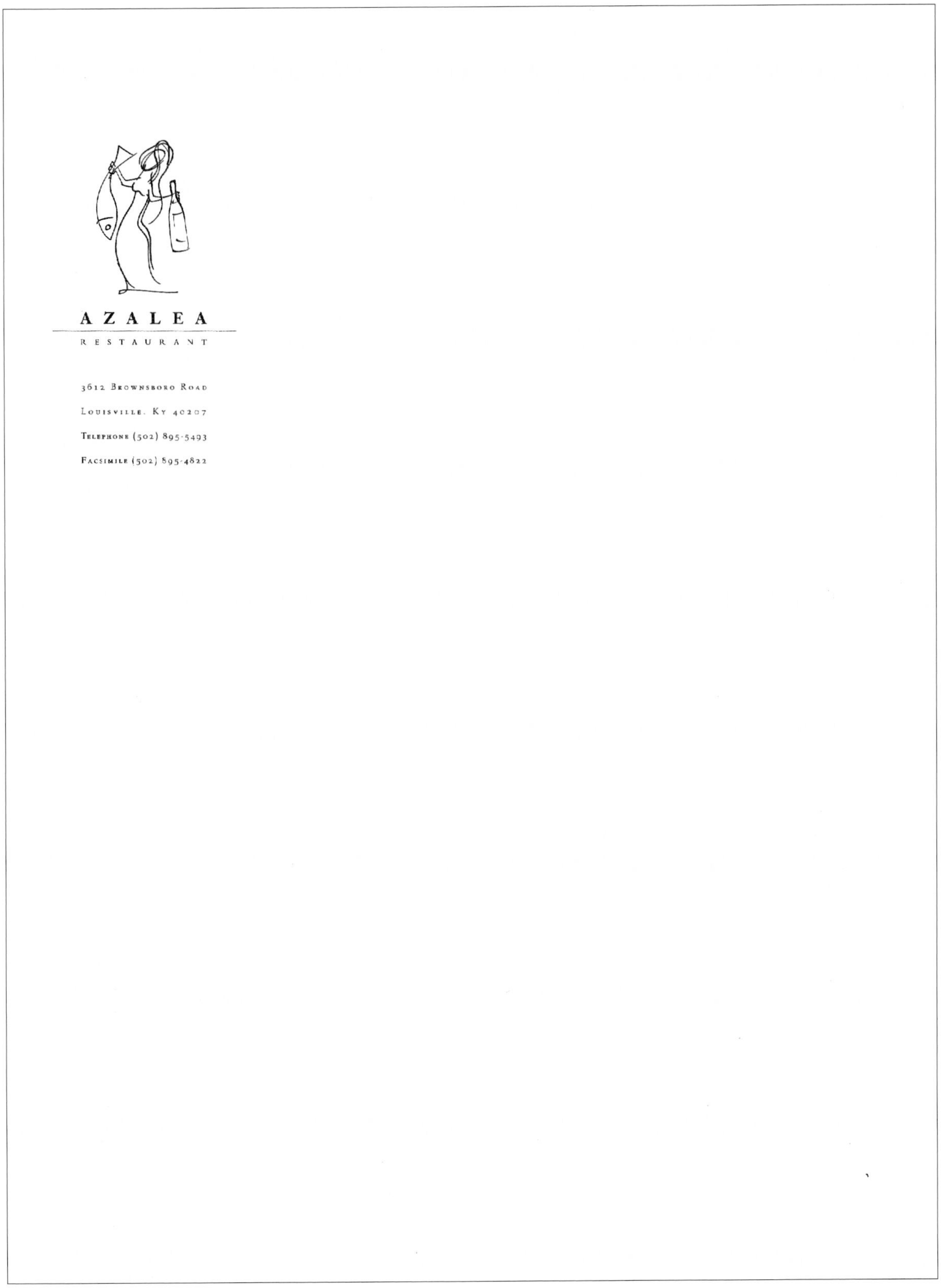

A Z A L E A

RESTAURANT

3612 BROWNSBORO ROAD

LOUISVILLE, KY 40207

TELEPHONE (502) 895-5493

FACSIMILE (502) 895-4822

design firm	Choplogic
art director	Walter McCord
designers	Walter McCord, Mary Cawein
client	Azalea
paper/printing	Simpson Antiqua/One-color lithography

COMMUNITY RELATIONS DEPT.

Target Stores   33 South Sixth Street   Minneapolis, MN 55402

COMMUNITY RELATIONS

Target Stores   33 South Sixth Street   Minneapolis, MN 55402

design firm	Design Guys
art director	Steven Sikora
designers	Anne Peterson, Tom Riddle
client	Target Stores
tool	Quark XPress
paper/printing	80 lb. Strathmore Writing/Challenge Printing

design firm	Vestígio
art director	Emanuel Barbosa
designer	Emanuel Barbosa
client	Latido
tool	Macromedia FreeHand
paper/printing	Renova Print/Two-color offset

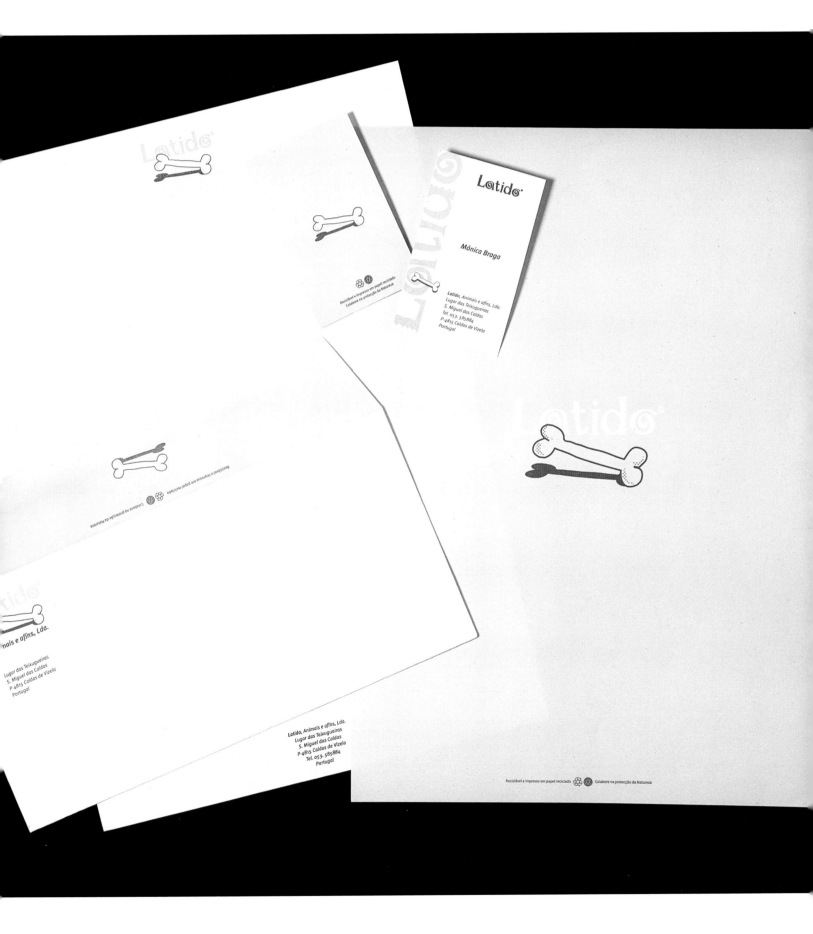

RALPH ALTHOFF

| Name: | | PHON | •49 (0) 821 - 59 29 58 |
| Adress: | Alpenstraße 18 | PHAX | •49 (0) 821 - 59 29 58 |

Alpenstraße 18	Bank	BfG Bank AG Augsburg
86159 Augsburg		BLZ 720 10 111
Germany		Kto 1422 6775 00

NO: 763

Logo:

RENT A BAR

Cocktails

≫ ≫ **RENT A BARMAN** • Ralph Althoff • Alpenstraße 18 • 86159 Augsburg

≫ **RENT A BAR VERANSTALTUNGSSERVICE** ≪

design firm	Marius Fahrner
art director	Marius Fahrner
designer	Marius Fahrner
client	'Rent a Bar' Barservice
tools	Adobe Illustrator, Quark XPress
paper/printing	Römerturm Countryside/
	Schickinger Werbedrull 2/0

design firm	Vrontikis Design Office
art director	Petrula Vrontikis
designers	Christina Hsaio, Stationary: Petrula Vrontikis
client	Kozo Hasegawa, Global Dining, Inc.
tools	Adobe Photoshop, Quark XPress
paper/printing	Crosspointe Synergy/Login Printing

1212 3rd Street Promenade

Santa Monica, CA 90401

fax: (310) 576-9988
www.global-dining.com

phone: (310) 576-9996

design firm	Mires Design
art director	John Ball
designers	John Ball, Miguel Perez, and Jeff Samaripa
client	dab fragrance sampling

D I V A N

7661 GIRARD AVE. LA JOLLA, CALIFORNIA 92037 **PH 619.551.0405 FAX 619.551.0639**

design firm	Miriello Grafico, Inc.
art director	Ron Miriello
designer	Courtney Mayer
client	Divan
tools	Adobe Illustrator, Adobe Photoshop, Macintosh
printing	Offset litho three color over two color

Boston Light Source
64 commercial wharf, Boston, Massachusetts 02110-3808

Architectural Lighting
Manufacturer's Repre

Boston Light Source
64 commercial wharf, Boston, MA 02110-3808

Boston Light Source
ROBERT A. EDWARDS
Architectural Lighting
Manufacturer's Representative
64 commercial wharf, Boston, MA 02110-3808
WEB: www.bostonlightsource.com
PHONE: 617.367.0910 x234 FAX: 617.367.0925
E-MAIL: redwards.bls@lighting.net

Boston Light Source
64 commercial wharf, Boston, MA 02110-3808

617.367.0910

FAX: 617.367.0925

WEB: www.bostonligl

Representing manufacturers offering products with a perceptible
advantage for the coordination of lighting with architecture.

design firm	**Korn Design**
art director	**Denise Korn**
designer	**Christine Brooks**
client	**Boston Light Source**
tools	**Adobe Illustrator, Quark XPress**
paper/printing	**Alpha Press**

HOOCH & HOLLY'S
SEASIDE BISTRO

P.O. BOX 1409
DOWNTOWN, ROUTE 1
OGUNQUIT, ME / 03907

T: (207) 646-HOOCH
F: (207) 646-5617

design firm	Korn Design
art director	Denise Korn
designers	Jenny Pelzek, Javier Cortés
client	Hooch & Holly's Restaurant
tools	Adobe Illustrator, Quark XPress, Macintosh Power PC
paper/printing	Classic Crest - Neenah/Alpha Press

recreation and entertainment

401 Richmond St.W. Suite 104   Toronto.Ontario.Canada M5V 1X3   phone (416)340-8869 fax 340-9819

design firm	**Cuppa Coffee Animation**
art director	**Adam Shaheen**
designer	**Julian Grey**
client	**Cuppa Coffee Animation**
paper/printing	**Central Printing**

design firm | **Brabender Cox**
art director | **Stephen Smith**
designer | **Stephen Smith**
client | **Breed Records**
tool | **Adobe Illustrator**

design firm | **what!design**
art director | **Damon Meibers**
designer | **Damon Meibers**
client | **Clearcut Recording**
tools | **Adobe Illustrator, Quark XPress**
paper/printing | **Atlas Printing**

design firm | **Blok Design**
art director | **Vanessa Eckstein**
designer | **Vanessa Eckstein**
client | **Industry Films**
tools | **Adobe Illustrator, Quark XPress**
paper/printing | **Strathmore Ultimate White/Offset**

design firm | Mires Design
art director | John Ball
designers | John Ball, Miguel Perez
illustrator | Tracy Sabin
client | Nike Inc.

design firm | Mires Design
art director | John Ball
designers | John Ball, Deborah Hom
client | Nike, Inc.

design firm	DogStar Design
art director	Jennifer Martin
designer	Jennifer Martin
client	Roaring Tiger Films
tool	Macromedia FreeHand

design firm	The Riordon Design Group, Inc.
art director	Ric Riordon
designers	Dan Wheaton, Sharon Porter
client	Free TV
tools	Adobe Illustrator, Quark XPress, Adobe Photoshop
paper/printing	Bravo/Contact Creative

design firm | **Iron Design**
art director | **Todd Edmonds**
designer | **Jim Keller**
client | **Ripcord Games**
tool | **Adobe Illustrator**
paper/printing | **Strathmore/Four-color process, metallic silver**

design firm | **Iron Design**
art director | **Todd Edmonds**
designer | **Ted Skibinski**
client | **PPI Entertainment**

design firm | **Mires Design**
art director | **Jose Serrano**
designers | **Jose Serrano, Miguel Perez**
client | **Hell Racer**

design firm | **Mires Design**
art director | **Jose Serrano**
designers | **Jose Serrano, Miguel Perez**
client | **Hell Racer**

design firm | **Jim Lange Design**
art director | **Kathleen Hughes**
designer | **Jim Lange**
client | **Public Library Association conference logo**
tool | **Macintosh**

design firm | **Karacters Design Group**
designer | **Maria Kennedy**
client | **Eaglequest Golf Centers**

Learn. Practice. Play.

eaglequest

Neil Lupkes
Maintenance

Pacific Golf
8080 Center Street S.W.
Tumwater
Washington
98501
Telephone:
(360) 786-8626
Facsimile:
(360) 786-8626
www.eaglequestgolf.com

Learn. Practice. Play.

actice. Play.

5419 Del Roy Drive

Dallas

Texas

75229

Direct Line:

(214) 706-6925

Facsimile:

(214) 706-6924

www.eaglequestgolf.com

Learn. Practice. Play.

design firm | **Art Chantry Design Company**
designer | **Art Chantry**
client | **Estrus Records**

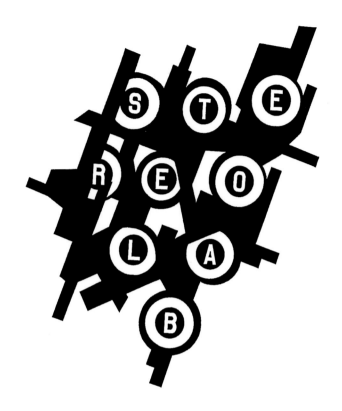

design firm | **Art Chantry Design Company**
designer | **Art Chantry**
client | **The Showbox**

design firm | **Art Chantry Design Company**
designer | **Art Chantry**
client | **Estrus Records**

design firm | **Art Chantry Design Company**
designer | **Art Chantry**
client | **Estrus Records**

design firm | **Art Chantry Design Company**
designer | **Art Chantry**
client | **Hell's Elevator Productions**

design firm | **Art Chantry Design Company**
designer | **Art Chantry**
client | **Empty Records**

design firm	Sametz Blackstone Associates
art director	Will Cook
designer	Will Cook
client	Provincetown Repertory Theatre
tools	Macintosh Power PC, Quark XPress, Adobe Photoshop, Infinity

MAMA
RECORDS

design firm	Vrontikis Design Office
art director	Petrula Vrontikis
designers	Victor Corpuz, Stationary: Winnie Li
client	Mama Records
tools	Quark XPress, Adobe Illustrator
paper/printing	Champion Benefit/Login Printing

THE LIONEL CORPORATION   50625 RICHARD W. BOULEVARD   TELEPHONE 810.949.4100   FACSIMILE 810.949.3273
CHESTERFIELD, MICHIGAN
48051-2493

design firm	**Michael Stanard Design**
art directors	**Michael Stanard, Marc Fuhrman**
designers	**Michael Chang, Marc Fuhrman**
client	**Lionel, LLC**
tools	**Adobe Illustrator, Macintosh**
paper/printing	**Strathmore Writing/**
	Offset lithography

DREAMS THAT ENDURE FOR GENERATIONS AND FUN THAT LASTS A LIFETIME

design firm	Jim Lange Design
art director	Jan Caille
designer	Jim Lange
client	Mrs. T's Chicago Triathlon
tools	Macintosh, Hand illustration
paper/printing	Smith Printing

design firm	Sametz Blackstone Associates
art director	Robert Beerman
designer	Hania Khuri
client	90.9 WBUR/The Connection
tools	Quark XPress, Adobe Photoshop, Macintosh Power PC
paper/printing	24 lb. Strathmore Writing Bright White/Puritan Press

90.9 WBUR
890 Commonwealth Avenue
Boston, Massachusetts
02215

617 353.2790
617 353.8147 fax

the connection

90.9 WBUR
Boston University
890 Commonwealth Avenue
Boston, Massachusetts
02215

the connection

CAMPAIGN CO

JJ Sutherland
Producer / Director

the conne

90.9 WBUR   617 353.0695
890 Commonwealth Ave. 617 353.5327 hotlin
Boston, Massachusetts   617 353.4747 fax
02215   jj.sutherland@wbur.

The Connection is a pro

design firm | Segura, Inc.
art director | Carols Segura
designer | Colin Metcalf
client | Q101 Radio
tools | Adobe Photoshop, Adobe Illustrator
paper/printing | MTG Productions

Festival Bay

design firm | Selbert Perkins Design
art director | Robin Perkins
design director | Greg Welch
designers | John Lutz, Ingrid Langhout, Julie D'Andrea
client | The Jerde Partnership International, Inc.

design firm | Selbert Perkins Design
art directors | Robin Perkins, Clifford Selbert
designers | Gemma Lawson, Heather Watson
client | The Jerde Partnership International, Inc.

70 UNIVERSAL CITY PLAZA   UNIVERSAL CITY, CALIFORNIA   USA   91608   818.777.4000 τ   WWW.MCARECORDS.COM

design firm	Segura, Inc.
art director	Carlos Segura
designers	Carlos Segura,
	Susana Detembleque
client	MCA
tools	Adobe Photoshop, Adobe Illustrator

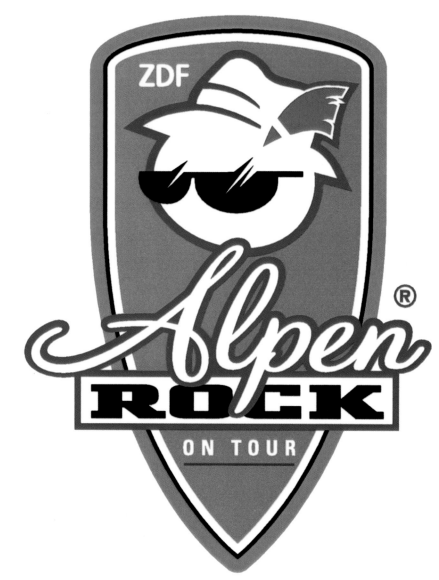

design firm | **Simon & Goetz Design**
art director | **Ruediger Goetz**
designer | **Ruediger Goetz**
illustrator | **Manuela Schmidt**
client | **ZDF**

design firm | Simon & Goetz Design
art director | Ruediger Goetz
designer | Ruediger Goetz
illustrator | Elke Boehm
client | ZDF

design firm | Simon & Goetz Design
art director | Ruediger Goetz
designers | Beth Martin, Jorge Waldschuetz
client | Helkon Media Filmvertries GMBH

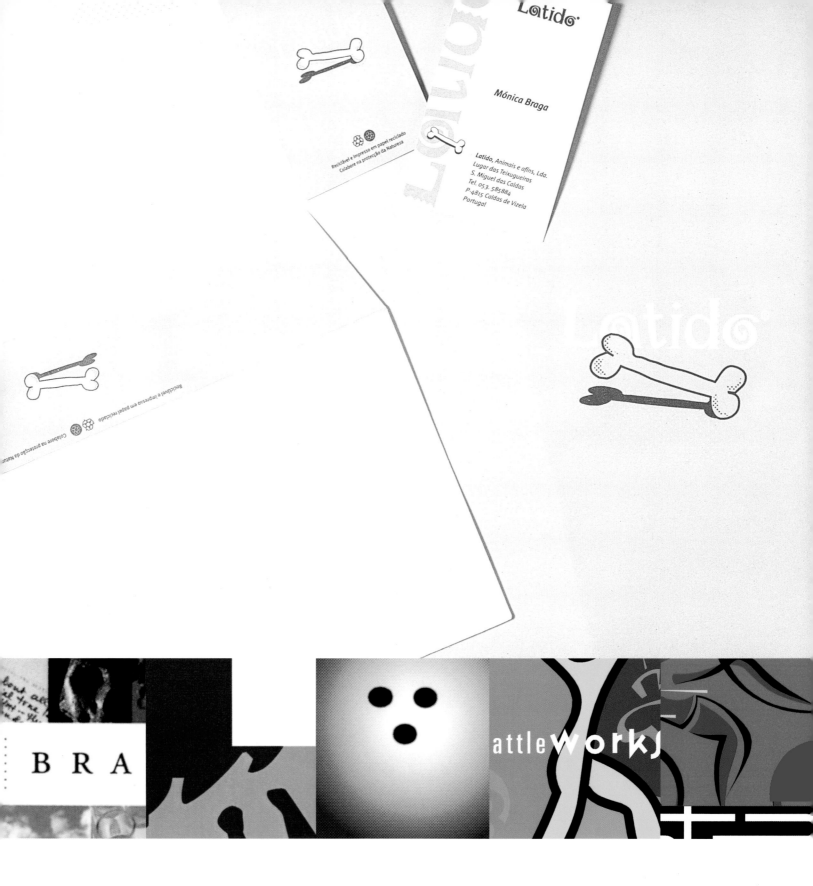

education, health,
and non-profit

SEATTLE TO PORTLAND BICYCLE CLASSIC

design firm | **That's Cadiz! Originals**
art director | **Mineleo Cadiz**
designer | **Mineleo Cadiz**
client | **Cascade Bicycle Club**
tool | **Macromedia FreeHand 8.0**

design firm | **That's Cadiz! Originals**
art director | **Mineleo Cadiz**
designer | **Mineleo Cadiz**
client | **Seattle Marathon Association**
tool | **Macromedia FreeHand 8.0**

273 East Erie Street Milwaukee Wisconsin 53202 **Phone** 414 276 7889 **Facsimile** 414 291 8078

Design Milwaukee
Milwaukee Institute of Art & Design

Building awareness of
design in Wisconsin

design firm	**Becker Design**
art director	**Neil Becker**
designer	**Neil Becker**
client	**Design Milwaukee**
tool	**Quark XPress**

Design Milwaukee
Milwaukee Institute of Art & Design

Building awareness of design in Wisconsin

design firm	Walker Pinfold Associates London
art director	Catherine Thomas
designer	Clare Wilson
client	Lampeter University-Australian Studies
tools	Quark XPress, Adobe Illustrator
paper/printing	Zanders Lana Graphic/Two-color lithography

design firm	Sayles Graphic Design
art director	John Sayles
designer	John Sayles
client	Goodtime Jazz Festival
tool	Macintosh
paper/printing	Neenah Bond/Offset

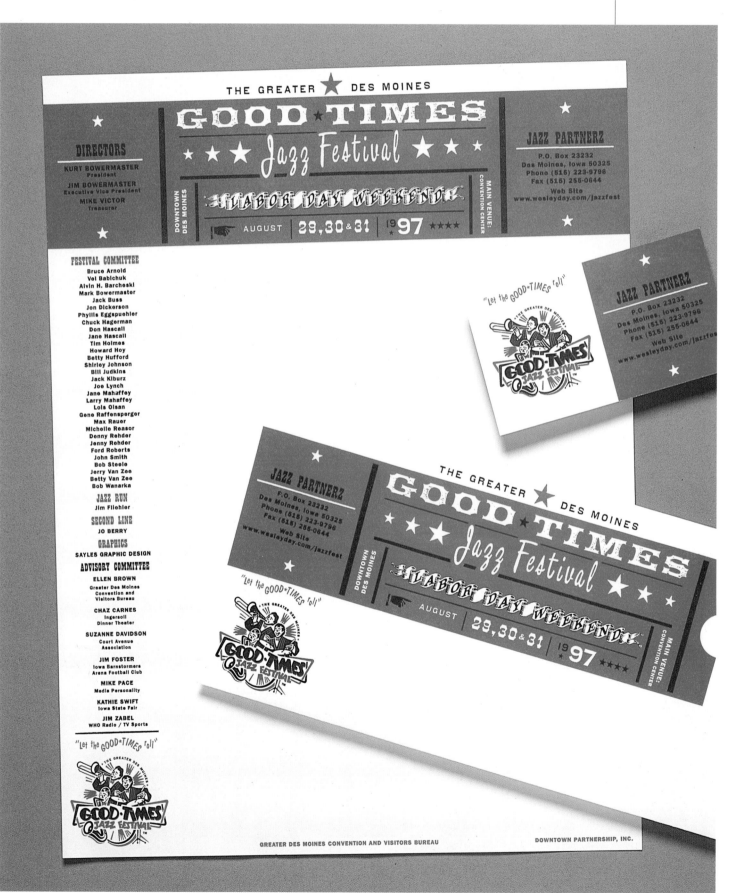

BOCATRIOL®

calcitriol

design firm | Leo Pharmaceutical Products
art director | Martin Isbrand
designer | Martin Isbrand
client | Leo Pharmaceutical Products

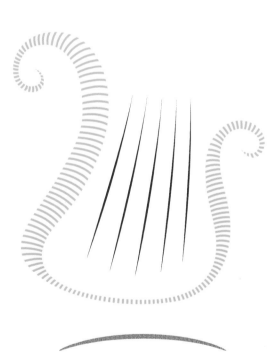

K L S O

design firm | Werk-Haus
designers | Ezrah Rahim, Paggie Chin Lee Choo
client | Kuala Lumpur Symphony Orchestra Society
tool | Macintosh

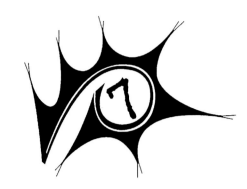

Seven Tepees Youth Program

design firm | Patricia Bruning Design
art director | Patricia Bruning
designers | Patricia Bruning, Fran Terry
client | Seven Tepees Youth Program
tools | Quark XPress 3.32, Adobe Illustrator 6.0,
Macintosh 7100 Power PC
paper/printing | Hamilton Press

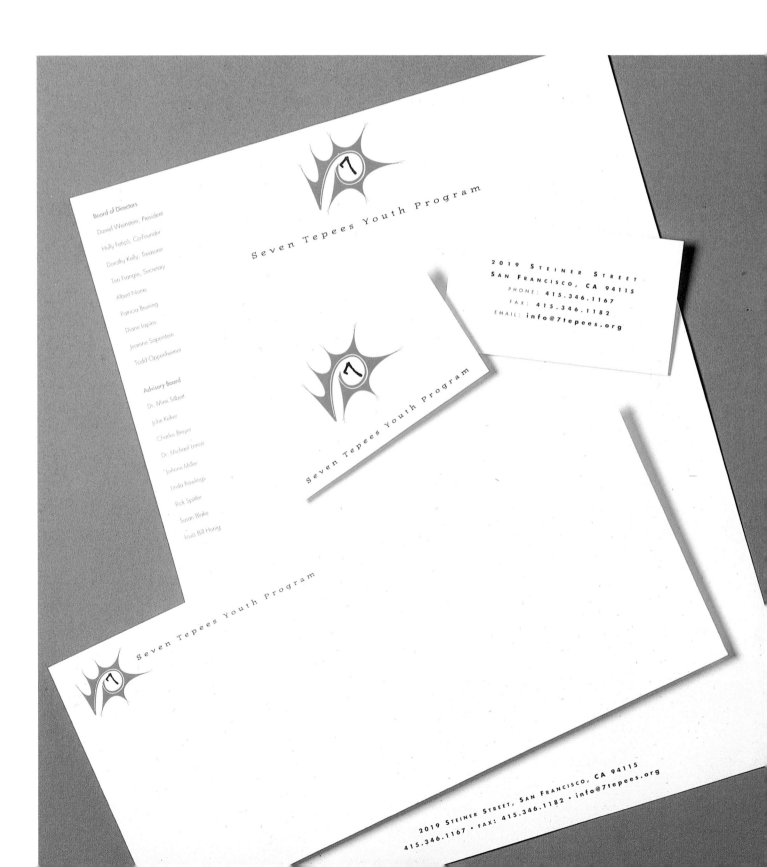

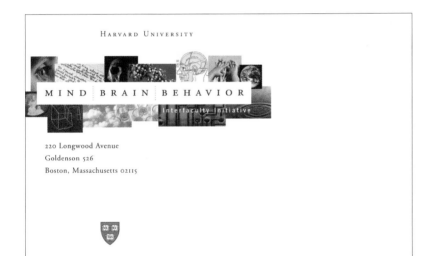

design firm	**Visual Dialogue**
art director	**Fritz Klaetke**
designers	**Fritz Klaetke, David Kraljic**
client	**Harvard University**
tools	**Quark XPress, Adobe Photoshop, Macintosh Power PC**
paper/printing	**Strathmore Elements/Color Express**

design firm | The Point Group
designer | David Howard
client | Big Brothers & Big Sisters of Dallas
tool | Adobe Illustrator

SUMMIT 1999

design firm | Leo Pharmaceutical Products
art director | Martin Isbrand
designer | Martin Isbrand
client | Leo Pharmaceutical Products

design firm	Vanderbyl Design
art director	Michael Vanderbyl
designers	Michael Vanderbyl, Erica Wilcott
client	The American Center for Wine, Food & the Arts
tools	Quark XPress, Adobe Illustrator
paper/printing	Cranes Crest/Trade Engraving

THE
AMERICAN
CENTER FOR
WINE FOOD
AND THE ARTS

PEGGY A. LOAR
DIRECTOR

THE
AMERICAN
CENTER FOR
WINE FOOD
AND THE
ARTS

FRANCES A. ANAMOSA
EXECUTIVE ASSISTANT
1700 SOSCOL AVE SUITE I NAPA CA 94559
TEL 707·257·3606 FAX 707·257·8601
EMAIL: fanamosa@theamericancenter.org

THE AMERICAN CENTER
FOR WINE, FOOD & THE ARTS
1700 SOSCOL AVENUE SUITE I
NAPA CALIFORNIA 94
TEL 707·257·3606 FAX 70

606 FAX 707·257·8601

design firm | **Sayles Graphic Design**
art director | **John Sayles**
designer | **John Sayles**
client | **Sue Roberts Health Concepts**
tool | **Macintosh**
paper/printing | **Neenah Environment Natural/Four-color offset**

design firm	That's Cadiz! Originals
art director	Mineleo Cadiz
designer	Mineleo Cadiz
client	Seattle Works
tool	Macromedia FreeHand 8.0

design firm | **Odeon Zwo**
art director | **Boris Eisenberg**
designer | **Dmitri Lavrow**
client | **Municipality of Hannover**

Landeshauptstadt **Hannover** | Referat für
Gleichstellungsfragen
Frauenbüro

Dienstgebäude | Röselerstraße 2 | 30159 Hannover

Referat für
Gleichstellungsfragen - Frauenbüro | Postfach 125 | 30001 Hannover

Bearbeitet von
TELEFON | 0511 **168** |
FAX | 0511 **168** | **6699**
Vermittlung | 0511 **168** | **0**

Sprechzeiten | dienstags | 15.00 - 17.00
| donnerstags | 09.00 - 12.00
| und nach Vereinbarung

Ihr Zeichen, Ihre Nachricht vom | Mein Zeichen (Bitte bei Antwort angeben) | Hannover
| 10.13/ |

Bankverbindungen der Stadtkasse	**BLZ**	**KONTO**
Stadtsparkasse Hannover	250 501 80	**517 321**
Deutsche Postbank AG Hannover	250 100 30	**15 - 305**
NordLB	250 500 00	**101 359 818**
Landeszentralbank in Niedersachsen	250 000 00	**250 017 68**

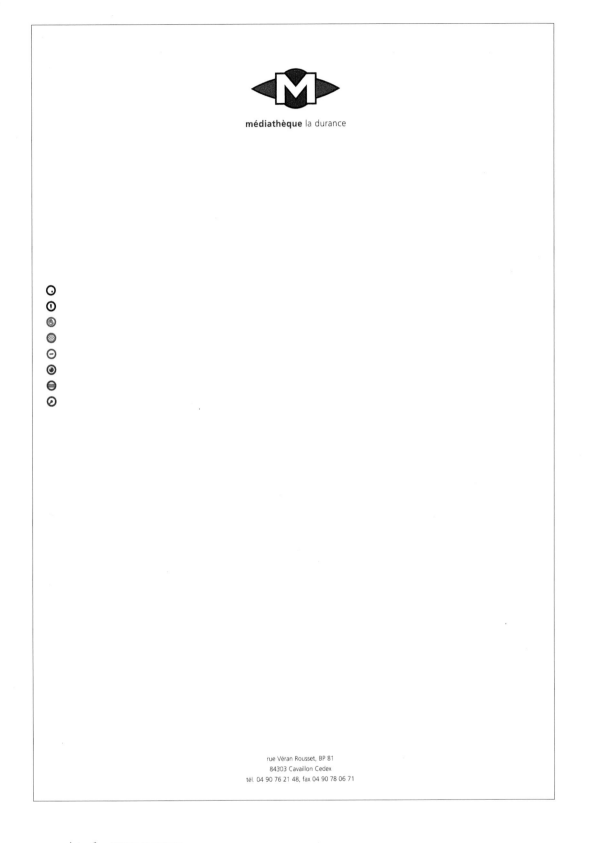

médiathèque la durance

rue Véran Rousset, BP 81
84303 Cavaillon Cedex
tél. 04 90 76 21 48, fax 04 90 78 06 71

design firm	**Made in mouse**
art director	**David Hairion**
designer	**Sandrine Langlet**
client	**Médiathèque de Cavaillon**
tools	**Macintosh Illustrator, Quark XPress**
paper/printing	**Rive/Offset**

miscellaneous

A M E R
I C A N
M A N I
C U R E

AMERICAN MANICURE CORPORATION
A DIVISION OF AM LABORATORIES, INC.
2328 CENTERLINE INDUSTRIAL DRIVE   ST. LOUIS, MO 63146   314.432.0363 FAX 432.8535 1.800.782.3555

design firm | Bartels & Company
art director | David Bartels
designers | Ron Rodemacher, Don Strandel
client | American Manicure
tools | Adobe Illustrator, Macintosh
paper/printing | Midwest Printing

LAURA KRETSCHMAR

A M E R
I C A N
M A N I
C U R E

2328 CENTERLINE INDUSTRIAL DR
ST.LOUIS, MO 63146   314.432.0363
FAX 314.432.8535 1.800.782.3555

design firm | Insight Design Communications
art directors | Tracy Holdeman, Sherrie Holdeman
designers | Tracy Holdeman, Sherrie Holdeman
client | Clotia Wood & Metal Works
tools | Macromedia FreeHand 7.0, Macintosh

design firm	Segura, Inc.
art director	Carlos Segura
designer	Carlos Segura
client	[T-26]
tool	Adobe Illustrator
paper/printing	Mohawk/Rohner Letterpress

design firm | **After Hours Creative**
designer | **After Hours Creative**
client | **Just One**

design firm	Synergy Design
designer	Leon Alvarado
client	Mega Estacíon
tools	Macromedia FreeHand,
	Macintosh
paper/printing	Various

THE FINE LINE

design firm	Murrie Lienhart Rysner
art director	Linda Voll
designer	Linda Voll
client	The Fine Line
tools	Adobe Illustrator

schwer **S** präzision

Schwer Präzision GmbH   Hauptstraße 148   D - 78588 Denkingen

Schwer Präzision GmbH	Telefon	Registergericht Tuttlingen	Kreissparkasse Spaichingen
Drehteile u. Techn. Produkte	07424 / 98 15-0	HRB 571 Sp. Sitz: Denkingen	643 500 70 Kto 455 095
Hauptstraße 148	Fax	Geschäftsführer: Klaus Schwer	Raiffeisenbank Denkingen
D - 78588 Denkingen	07424 / 98 15-30	USt.-Id.-Nr. DE 811731829	643 626 13 Kto 50 444 000

design firm	**revoLUZion**
art director	**Bernd Luz**
designer	**Bernd Luz**
client	**Schwer Präzision**
tools	**Macromedia FreeHand, Macintosh**

design firm | Russell, Inc.
art director | Bob Russell
client | Cancom, Inc.

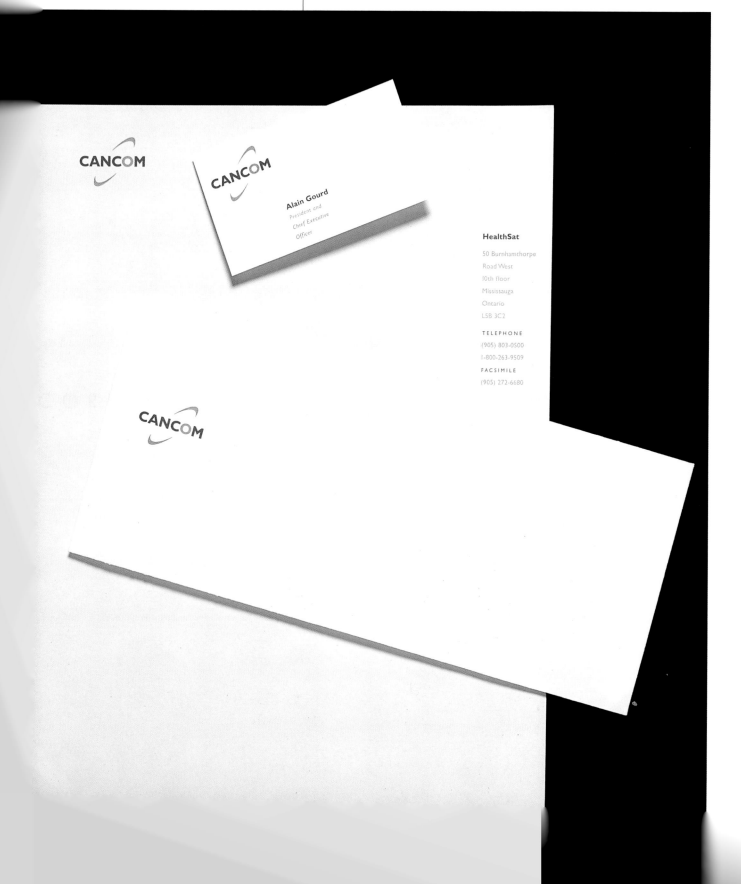

design firm | Segura, Inc.
art director | Carlos Segura
designer | Carlos Segura
client | Blue Rock
tools | Adobe Photoshop, Adobe Illustrator

DETERMAN BROWNIE, INC.

· 1241 72ND AVENUE NORTHEAST
MINNEAPOLIS, MN 55432

PHONE: 612.571.8110

FAX: 612.571.1789

design firm | Design Center
art director | John Reger
designer | Jon Erickson
client | Determan Brownie, Inc.
tools | Macromedia FreeHand,
| Macintosh
paper/printing | Strathmore Writing/
| Wallace Carlson

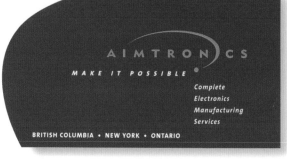

design firm	Big Eye Creative
art directors	Perry Chua, Nancy Yeasting
designers	Perry Chua, Nancy Yeasting
client	Aimtronics Corporation
tools	Adobe Illustrator, Macintosh Power PC
paper/printing	Cards: McCoy Silk, Rest: Classic Printing

**AIMTRONICS
CORPORATION**

100 Schneider Road
Kanata, Ontario
Canada K2K 1Y2
tel 613.592.2240
fax 613.592.9449

ONTARIO

NEW YORK

BRITISH COLUMBIA

AIMTRON CS

MAKE IT POSSIBLE

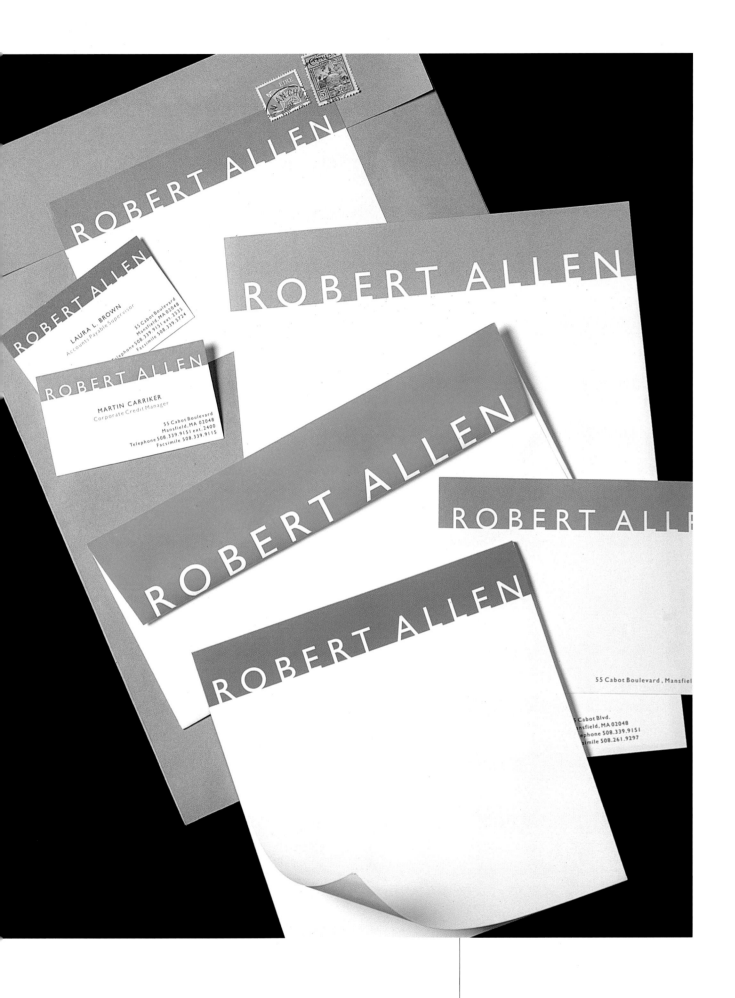

design firm	Slover and Company
art director	Susan Slover
designer	Tamara Behar
client	Robert Allen Contract Fabrics
tools	Adobe Illustrator, Quark XPress, Macintosh Power PC
paper/printing	Two-color offset

design firm | **Patricia Bruning Design**
art director | **Patricia Bruning**
designers | **Patricia Bruning, Fran Terry**
client | **Johnson Hoke**
tools | **Quark XPress 3.32, Adobe Illustrator 6.0,**
Macintosh 7100 Power PC
paper/printing | **Golden Dragon Printing**

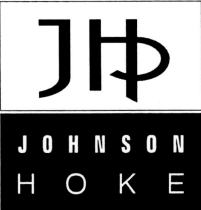

design firm	Stewart Monderer Design, Inc.
art director	Stewart Monderer
designer	Aime Lecusay
client	NBase-Xyplex
tools	Adobe Illustrator, Macintosh G3

JUNOVIA

design firm	**Robert Bailey Incorporated**
art director	**Dan Franklin**
designers	**Dan Franklin, Connie Lightner**
client	**Junovia Distributing**
tools	**Macromedia FreeHand 7.0, Quark XPress**
paper/printing	**Classic Crest/ Michael's Printing**

JUNOVIA

JUNOVIA DISTRIBUTING, LLC
DISTRIBUTOR *of* PREMIUM CIGARS & ACCESSORIES

8048 SW EDGEWATER DRIVE WEST ❚ WILSONVILLE, OREGON 97070 ❚ 503 694.6620 *tel* ❚ 503 694.5094 *fax*

design firm | **Cynthia Patten**
art director | **Cynthia Patten**
designer | **Cynthia Patten**
client | **Eye D**
tools | **Quark XPress 3.32, Adobe Illustrator 6.0,**
Macintosh 7100 Power PC
paper/printing | **French Paper Frostone (Iceberg)/**
Epson Ink Jet

IVR Rohloff An der Schluse 23 D-48329 Havixbeck

Industrie-Vertretung
Rohloff

An der Schluse 23
D-48329 Havixbeck

Tel. 0 25 07 - 44 99
Fax 0 25 07 - 13 05

Vertrieb elektronischer
Geräte und Systeme

design firm	**revoLUZion**
art director	**Bernd Luz**
designer	**Bernd Luz**
client	**IVR Rohloff**
tools	**Macromedia Freehand, Macintosh**

design firm | **revoLUZion**
art director | **Bernd Luz**
designer | **Bernd Luz**
client | **revoLUZion/self**
tools | **Adobe Photoshop, Quark XPress, Macintosh**

design firm | **Elixir Design, Inc.**
art director | **Jennifer Jerde**
designer | **Nathan Durant**
client | **Perspecta**
tool | **Adobe Illustrator**

design firm | **Elixir Design, Inc.**
art director | **Jennifer Jerde**
designer | **Nathan Durant**
client | **Athleta**
tool | **Adobe Illustrator**

design firm | Towers Perrin - Creative Media Group
art director | Jim Kohler
designer | Geoff Stone
client | Towers Perrin
tools | Quark Xpress, Adobe Photoshop,
Adobe Illustrator, Macintosh

directory

**AC/DC—Art Chantry
Design Company**
P.O. Box 4069
Seattle, WA 98104

Acro Media, Inc.
431 Highway 33
Kelowna, BC
Canada

After Hours Creative
1201 East Jefferson B100
Phoenix, AZ 85034

Anne Gordon Design Pty. Ltd.
1 Caledonia Street
Paddington NSW 2021
Australia

Arrowstreet Graphic Design
212 Elm Street
Somerville, MA 02144

Art-Direction & Design
Schröderstiftstrasse 28
20146 Hamburg
Germany

Barabara Chan Design
614 South Saint Andrews, Suite 409
Los Angeles, CA 90005

Bartels and Company
3284 Ivanhoe Avenue
St. Louis, MO 63139

Becker Design
225 East St. Paul Avenue, Suite 300
Milwaukee, WI 53202

Belyea
1809 7th Avenue
Seattle, WA 98101

Big Eye Creative
101-1300 Richards Street
Vancouver, BC V68 3G6
Canada

Blok Design
398 Adelaide West, Suite 602
Toronto, Ontario M5V 2K4
Canada

Blue i Design
Imperial House
Lypiatt Road
Cheltenham GL50 2QJ
UK

Bob's Haus
3728 McKinley Boulevard
Sacramento, CA 95816

Brabender Cox
2100 Wharton Street
Pittsburgh, PA 15203

Choplogic
2014 Cherokee Parkway
Louisville, KY 40204

Cuppa Coffee Animation, Inc.
401 Richmond Street West, #104
Toronto, Ontario M5V IX3
Canada

Customized Communications Group
975 Middle Street, Suite B
Middletown, CT 06457

Design Center
15119 Minnetonka Boulevard
Mound, MN 55364

Design Guys
119 North Fourth Street, #400
Minneapolis, MN 55401

Designstudio CAW
Krugstrasse 16
30453 Hannover
Germany

DogStar Design
626 54th Street South
Birmingham, AL 35203

Earthlink Creative Services
3100 New York Drive
Pasadena, CA 91107

Ellis Pratt Design, Inc.
361 Newbury Street
Boston, MA 02115

**Focus Design
and Marketing Solutions**
3800 Valley Lights Drive
Pasadena, CA 91107

Giorgio Rocco Communications
Via Domenichino 27
20149 Milano
Italy

Gouthier Design
P.O. Box 840925
Hollywood, FL 33084

Grafik Communications, Ltd.
1199 North Fairfax Street, Suite 700
Alexandria, VA 22314

Greteman Group
142 North Mosley, 3rd Floor
Witchita, KS 67209

Hamagami/Carroll & Associates
1316 3rd Street
Promenade, #305
Santa Monica, CA 90401

Han/Davis Group
2933 North Sheridan, Apt. 1417
Chicago, IL 60657

Henderson Tyner Art Co.
315 N. Spruce Street, Suite 299
Winston-Salem, NC 27101

Hornall Anderson Design Works, Inc.
1008 Western Avenue, Suite 600
Seattle, WA 98104

Iconix Group
4927 Auburn Avenue
Bethesda, MD 20814

Insight Design Communication
322 South Mosley
Wichita, KS 67202

Iron Design
120 North Aurora Street, Suite 5A
Ithaca, NY 14850

Jim Lange Design
203 North Wabash Avenue
Chicago, IL 60601

João Machado Design, Lda
Rua Padre Xavier Coutinho,
125, 4150-371 Porto
Portugal

Karacters Design Group
1600-777 Hornby
Vancouver, BC
Canada

Kirima Design Office
5F, 1-5, Park-Bild, Yorikimachi
Yorikimachi, Kita-ku, Osaka-City
530-0036
Japan

Korn Design
22 Follen Street
Boston, MA 02116

Laughlin/Winkler, Inc.
4 Clarendon Street
Boston, MA 02116

Leo Pharmaceutical Products
Industriparken 55
Ballerup 2750
Denmark

Lima Design
215 Hanover Street
Boston, MA 02113

Lux Design
550 15th Street, #25A
San Francisco, CA 94103

Made in mouse
Moulin Priaulet BP 32
13520 Maussane
France

Marius Fahrner
Lastropsweg 5
20255 Hamburg
Germany

McGaughy Design
3706-A Steppes Court
Falls Church, VA 22041

Michael Stanard Design
1000 Main Street
Evanston, IL 60202

Mires Design
2345 Kettner Boulevard
San Diego, CA 92101

Modelhart Grafik-Design DA
A-5600 St. Johann/Pg Ing.
Ludwig Pech Str. 7
Austria

Moonlight Press Studio
362 Cromwell Avenue
Staten Island, NY 10305

Murrie Lienhart Rysner
325 West Huron Street
Chicago, IL 60607

Nesnady & Schwartz
10803 Magnolia Drive
Cleveland, OH 44106

Never Boring Design
1016 14th Street
Modesto, CA 95354

Nielinger Kommunikations design
Borsig str.5
45145 Essen
Germany

Oakley Design Studio
519 South West Park Avenue, Suite 521
Portland, OR 97205

Odeon Zwo
Odeonstr.2
D-30 59 Hannover
Germany

Parachute Design
120 S. 6th Street
Minneapolis, MN 55402

Patricia Bruning Design
1045 Sansome Street, Suite 219
San Francisco, CA 94111

Patten Design
55 Queensberry Street
Boston, MA 02215

Pham Phu Design
Hohenzollernstr.97
Munich 80796
Germany

Philips Design Group
25 Drydock Avenue
Boston, MA 02210

Planet Design Company
605 Williamson Street
Madison, WI 53703

Plum Notion Design Laboratory
140 Huyshope Avenue
Hartford, CT 06106

Prime Studio
326 7th Avenue
New York, NY 10001

Q Design
Neuberg 14
65193 Wiesbaden
Germany

revoLUZion
Uhlandstr. 4
78579 Neuhausen
Germany

Richards Design Group
5616 Kingston Park
Knoxville, TN 37919

Riordan Design Group
131 George Street
Oakville, Ontario
Canada

Robert Bailey, Inc.
0121 South West Bancroft Street
Portland, OR 97201

Roslyn Eskind Associates
471 Richmond Street West
Toronto, Ontario
Canada

Russell, Inc.
119 Spadina Avenue, Level 5,
Toronto, Ontario, M5V 2L1
Canada

Sametz Blackstone Associates
40 W. Newton Street
Boston, MA 02118

Sayegh Design
24734 Independence Drive, #3111
Farmington, MI 48333

Sayles Graphic Design
308 8th Street
Des Moines, IA 50309

Scott Stern
8 Minerva Way
Glasgow G38AU
UK

Segura, Inc.
1110 N. Milwaukee Avenue
Chicago, IL 60622

Seltzer Design
30 The Fenway
Boston, MA 02215

Shook Design Group
2000 South Boulevard, Suite 510
Charlotte, NC 28204

Slover and Company
584 Broadway, Suite 903
New York, NY 10001

Spin Productions, Inc.
620 King Street West
Totonto, Ontario
Canada

Square One Design
970 Monroe Avenue Northwest
Grand Rapids, MI 49503

Steven Curtis Design, Inc.
1807 West Sunnyside
Chicago, IL 60640

Stewart Monderer Design, Inc.
10 Thacher Street, Suite 112
Boston, MA 02113

Stoltze Design
49 Melcher Street, 4th Floor
Boston, MA 02210

Studio Bubblan
7:E Villagatan 28
50454 Boras
Sweden

Studio Hill: Design Ltd.
417 Second Street SW,
Ald. NM 87102
Synergy Design
600 Nottingham Oaks, #279
Houston, TX 77079

Synergy Design
600 Nottingham Oaks, Suite 279
Houston, TX 77079

Teviot
7 Dublin Street Lane South
Edinburgh EH1 3PX
UK

That's Cadiz! Originals
3823 14th Avenue West
Seattle, WA 98101

The Point Group
5949 Sherry Lane, Suite 1800
Dallas, TX 75225

Vanderbyl Design
171 2nd Street
San Francisco, CA 94109

Vestígio
Av. Sidónio Pais, 379,
Salas 4-5 P-4100 Porto
Portugal

Visual Dialogue
429 Columbus Avenue #1,
Boston, MA 02116

Vrontikis Design Office
2021 Pontius Pilot Avenue
Los Angeles, CA 90025

Walker Pinfold Associates London
17, The Ivories 6 Northampton Street
London NI 2HY
UK

Walker Thomas Associates
Top Floor, Osment Buildings
Maples Lane Prahran 3181
Australia

Warren Group
622 Hampton Drive
Venice, CA 90231

Werk-Haus
71-3 Medan Setia 1 Bukit Damansara
50490 Kuala Lumpur
Malaysia

what!design
119 Braintree
Allston, MA 02134

Woodworth Associates
151 Newbury Street
Portland, ME 04101

X Design Company
2525 West Main Street, #201
Littleton, CO 80120

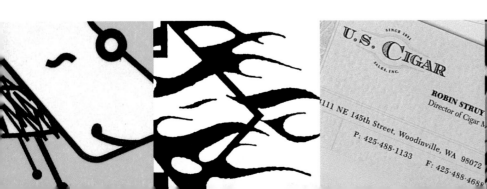

index